Stupid Boat Tricks

Stupid Boat Tricks

and other terrible tales of the bounding main

by John Kenneth Bruce

Momentum Books, Ltd.
Troy, Michigan

Copyright © 1999 Great Lakes Cruiser, Inc.

All rights reserved. No part of this book may be used or reproduced in any manner without prior written permission of the publisher except in the case of brief quotations embodied in critical reviews and articles.

Manufactured in the United States of America

2001   2000   1999   3   2   1

1-879094-63-0

Momentum Books, Ltd.
1174 E. Big Beaver Rd.
Troy, Michigan 48083

This book is dedicated to my lovely wife who has stood by me through all kinds of weather, both afloat and ashore...

Contents

Dedication	v
Foreword	xi
Stuck with the Trailer	1
Are We There Yet?	5
The Rights of Spring	8
The Fine Art of Docking	10
Winter Cruising? A Letter for the Men:	13
What's Under the Tarp?	16
J.K.'s Law	20
Wild Bill Hiccup and the T-Bone	24
"Annie, Forget the Gun…"	27
Babes in Toyland	32
When in Rome…	35
Part of an Old, Dead Bird…	37
The Sins of Our Fathers…	41
The Brave Little Ducks	46
Do Not Read 'til All Hallow's Eve…	49
With Apologies…	53
Unindicted Co-Conspirators	56
When the Captain Tossed His Cookies…	60
Nauticalese…	63
The Great Trailer Chase	67
My Blue Poly	71
So What's for Dinner?	74
Four-Legged Cruisers	77

Walking in a Winter Wonderland...	80
Lose Your Breakfast at Tiffany's	84
Night of The Beagle	86
Burnt Offerings	91
They'll Always Come Out to Get You...	95
Commander Ma'am	98
The Survivalist	102
The Flare	105
All Hail, Sony...	109
You Can Always Count on the Coast Guard...	114
Faster than a Speeding Bullet...	116
"It Was Quicker This Way..."	119
Rub-A-Dub-Dub...	122
The Day It Hit the Fan...	126
Look Who's Driving!	130
Dilbert Groggins and the Crime of the Century	134
The Finer Art of Anchoring	140
The All-Seeing Oz...	144
Practice Makes Perfect	147
Navigation: the Winter Rules	150
Me, My Wife & That Darn Ghost!	153
Let's All Do the Mast Step...	158
A Bridge Too Far...	162
Dad Will Never Know...	167
"I'll Run Circles Around Ya!"	171
The Political Season	175
The Big Switch	178
What's in a Name?	182
The Fashion Bug	184
For the Want of a Boom Box...	187
Dick and Jane at the Boat Show	191
Politically Correct Cruising	193
Christmas, Most of All	196
Boating by the Seat of Your Pants	198
I Think She's Trying to Kill Me...	202

Stupid Boat Tricks

Is There Sound in a Vacuum?	205
Parts Is Parts...	210
Pompeii Pumpout	213
Picture This...	217

Foreword

It all started one Fourth of July a few years ago. Several of us staff members from *Great Lakes Cruiser Magazine* were enjoying a long, holiday weekend at the home port. We don't like going out on the bay on busy weekends like this. Who wants to fight the waters filled with the "rude, crude and stewed" holiday crowd when you can sit safely in port? Nope, we wrote this weekend off and opted to sit in the cockpit of Chuck & Sue's boat and share a few beers.

Beer is a wonderful substance. Before long we started swapping stories about our most embarrassing boating moments. We all have them, those little incidents that happened so very long ago but somehow... never go away. We dubbed them "Stupid Boat Tricks" on the spot and everybody took a turn. As good friends as we all were, I can't remember our ever having had a better time together than that afternoon. This Stupid Boat Trick stuff was magic!

As long as the beer kept flowing, so did the stories. But what no one realized was that I was taking notes. In all honesty I thought this would make a great topic for my column in the magazine and if I was real careful, I might be able to bleed this material for four or five months... that was nearly five years ago. And let me tell you the most wonderful thing about Stupid Boat Tricks: When you tell one, people will tell you five more!

John Kenneth Bruce

Since then I have shared a great number of these boating atrocities with our readers, and their regular appearance in the pages of *Great Lakes Cruiser* have apparently become something to look forward to. Here in this book are the stories of New Guy Navigator, Captain Crunch and Dr. X. Here are incidents with drawbridges, boat trailers, and flare guns (devices designed to embarrass and befuddle us). Here are tales of endurance under adverse conditions like motors that go into business for themselves, marine toilets that explode and barbecued sacrifices to the gods.

The bottom line is, if it happened to a boater and it's funny, it's probably in this book. Enjoy...

But this book is designed for you to enjoy for two reasons: 1. Yes, this is proof that there is someone else out there who has done it worse than you, and 2. Apparently no one saw you when you did yours. But relax, even if we did see you, your name and the circumstances were changed to protect your identity and our liability.

So here they are, every Stupid Boat Trick story I ever wrote (so far) and a nice collection of my other favorite pieces. Learn by these examples, benefit from these experiences and laugh when no one's watching...

Mr. Bruce's Column appears monthly in *Great Lakes Cruiser Magazine*. For more information, visit:
http://www.concentric.net/~Glcruise or call: 248-545-5999.

Stuck with the Trailer

Several years back, Bruce Jenvey bought his own first "serious" boat. It was a twenty-four foot, trailerable sailboat with just enough room for the family and lots of room for improvement. It came complete with a large, heavy-duty, "bunk-style" trailer. You know, no rollers...just big, wooden, felt-covered, bunks curved to cradle the bottom of the boat. The boat also had something else: a very slight case of hull blisters. Well, Jenvey spent the winter reading about how to take care of those babies and at the first sign of spring, he was in the backyard, under the trailer, chipping, sanding, fairing and sealing.

It was not an easy process but one that was done completely. With the help of his friends, Jenvey jacked the boat up off of the trailer bunks and onto blocks to best expose the bottom. After the bottom was sanded, sealed in fresh epoxy, bottom painted and allowed to properly cure, the boat was again lowered back on to the trailer and those spots concealed by the blocks were given the same treatment.

Finally, it was launch day! Jenvey had rented a marina slip out along the north shore of Lake St. Clair and all that was left to do, was take the boat to the water. Down the street, friendly neighbor "Doc" Jim (a young radiologist in his last year of residency) offered the services of himself and his 4x4 for the towing-launching ceremonies. So off they went that unseasonably warm spring day; Jenvey, Doc Jim and the twenty-four foot wonder boat.

At the launching ramp, the marina operator warned them that since this was such a low-water year, he had concerns over their ability to launch a sailboat at the ramp. He quite frankly admitted he didn't know how much water was down there. But after watching a few of the larger fishing boats come and go without difficulty, they decided to give it a try.

Doc Jim backed the trailer down the ramp with great expertise to the point where the truck's rear tires nearly touched the water and yes...they could see by the angle of the water along the boat's hull that this indeed was a pretty shallow ramp. The trailer's fenders and illuminated taillights were still very visible just under the water. The pair tried to push the boat off the trailer bunks (remember, no rollers) and into the water but it was no good, they just weren't deep enough.

"Back it in further," Jenvey shouted as he waved the 4x4 into the water up to the hub caps, but still there was not enough water to free the boat from the trailer. "More, more!" he directed as Doc Jim backed the truck down the ramp as far as he possibly dared, to the point where the exhaust was literally blowing bubbles. But still they were in shallow water. The strength of two grown men precariously standing on the trailer tongue was not enough to shove the boat off the bunks. Closer inspection from the dock showed the trailer fenders and tail lights still visible and still painfully close to the surface of the water.

Frustration set in. "Now what?" they wondered as they started to formulate alternative launching plans. Deep in thought, Jenvey leaned against the boat's stern from his standing position on the dock. To his amazement, the boat moved! It rocked gently and effortlessly as it slid sideways away from them. But just below the surface of the water, those cursed trailer fenders and tail lights were also bobbing, rocking and sliding away. The entire apparatus was floating!

Apparently epoxy curing times in cold spring weather take far longer than even the manufacturer had anticipated, and the general result was that Jenvey had glued his trailer to the bottom of his boat. After the initial shock and the obvious comments about how convenient this could turn out to be (hey, water levels were low and there were a lot of sandbars just below the surface out there!), reality set in for both men that here, they faced a truly embarrassing situation. How does one get the trailer unglued from the bottom of one's boat without anyone knowing what you're doing.

Luck was with them since no one was waiting for the ramp. There were only a handful of people in the vicinity working on their boats and a crew of carpenters working on the new deck for the marina's restaurant. Doc Jim immediately kicked off his shoes, rolled up his jeans and put one foot on the dockside trailer fender instantly discovering what Jenvey already knew: while the air was an unseasonable 75 degrees, the water, freshly down the river from Lake Huron was a mere 42. The boat and trailer listed slightly, but refused to part company.

Gritting his teeth, Doc Jim supported himself between the dock piling and a stanchion and bravely put both feet on the fender...nothing. A few words as blue as Doc Jim's feet were exchanged and it was decided that they would both have to stand on a trailer fender...but since it was Jenvey's boat, Doc Jim would get the position on the fender he already guarded. Jenvey would have to lower himself over the side to the other fender, hanging from a stanchion, and more than likely get dunked when the trailer finally let go. Doc Jim pointed out that it's the responsibility of the captain to go down with his ship, or his trailer, whichever sinks first.

Doc Jim shivered atop his own fender while verbally

encouraging Jenvey to hurry up and get on top of his own on the other side. But as Jenvey lowered himself towards the water and barely put the pressure of one toe on the starboard side trailer fender, the entire trailer unexpectedly let loose and dropped to the bottom like a gallows.

Luckily for Jenvey, he was still hanging on quite tightly to the stanchion and managed to pull himself back up to the deck without getting more than a couple of toes wet. Doc Jim, however, didn't fair so well. The sudden drop caught him by surprise and he rode his fender all the way to the bottom leaving him waist-deep in 42 degree water.

Jenvey later said that the agonizing scream that emanated from the young doctor involved expletives that only a physician would use. This, of course, attracted the attention of everyone in the general vicinity. Fortunately, all of the witnesses immediately drew the conclusion that Doc Jim had simply fallen in…it happens. No one present ever found out that Jenvey had glued his trailer to the bottom of his boat.

Are We There Yet?

How many times have we heard that while driving along the highway to Grandma's house? I don't know about you, but there are times those four little words can turn me into the original Big Bad Wolf. And if those don't get me, the ones that follow certainly will: "What time will we get there?" and "What time is it now?"

Can't these kids see we're still driving? Can't they tell time on their own? Didn't we buy them watches last Christmas? I realize they ask these questions because they have become bored. But how could they become so bored in the car?

Here they are, whizzing along at 75 miles per hour…or slightly less depending on who's watching, with constantly changing scenery, road signs flying by and other cars with other kids passing and making silly faces. They have hundreds of dollars worth of portable electronic entertainment equipment back there. How could they be bored?

And then a very frightening thought may occur to you, as it did to me: If they're this bored at these sensational speeds, with all this dashing scenery, what are they going to be like on the long cruise you've planned for this summer?

Think about it. You'll be whizzing along at maybe 50 miles an hour slower. And if you're a sailor, you may not be whizzing along at all! You'll be several miles off shore which makes the scenery seem to barely crawl past. And there won't be another boat within a mile or so, which can be an advantage when you realize that all the eye witnesses are too far away to make a positive ID should things become desperate. And when the kids have worn out their batteries and have tired of playing with that funny toilet you have on the boat, they will suddenly throw those magic words at you...Let's not say them, instead, let's talk about ways to prevent them!

The object is to keep the kids busy, give them something to do that will keep their devious little minds occupied. I've compiled my own time-tested list over the years. I'll share it with you now so that you can be best prepared to make your summer cruise a success.

> 1. As you enter unfamiliar waters, tell them how important it is that someone watch for U-Boats. You're too busy driving.

> 2. If your cruise finds you in Lake Erie, have them watch for the infamous sea monster instead. Of course you realize they will spot it...about a hundred times a day.

> 3. Offer free passes for the Keel Haul Ride.

> 4. Inflate the dinghy and tow them behind you on the longest line you have on board.

> 5. Let them drive, then sit directly behind them and repeatedly tell them how it's done. Better yet, ask them if we're there yet.

Seriously, if you're going to cruise, cruising with children may be a reality and you can improve your own enjoyment of this time by improving theirs. And sometimes, it really

Stupid Boat Tricks

doesn't take that much! I was serious about letting them take the helm. The kids love to drive and it might give you a chance to enjoy the scenery a little bit too. Find other jobs and other responsibilities they can shoulder. This can make them more a part of the crew and less a part of the baggage compartment. When my kids were younger, I had them all learn coastal piloting and chart work and had them recheck my navigation, and in many cases, I just left the course plotting to them!

Also, remember you're on vacation. I have a small TV on board and I know folks who actually have a VCR too. Let the kids watch TV! At least for a few days, throw out the silly rules about how many hours a day they can watch. Let them take in the fresh air when they want and let them vegetate below as they wish, too…as long as you're underway, that is.

The important thing here is they aren't chattel slaves. Chattel slaves become unhappy and when they're unhappy, you're miserable. This could be a great time to share together and the better it is, the more often you may find yourself doing it.

The Rights of Spring

We, the boaters, the cruisers and the warm weather recreators of the Great Lakes Region declare that certain unalienable Rights exist to protect our kind, ensure our season and preserve our sanity. That the boating season shall commence and these Rights shall become enforceable each and every April 2nd, for to do so even one day earlier would be foolish. That these Rights shall supersede all previous claims, designs and accumulated precipitation regardless of quantity, quality and date of deposit. We hereby find these Rights to be long over due:

By April 2nd of every year, any remaining ice in any marina shall be broken, removed and be served to us in our martinis, iced tea and Mountain Dew. To perform this public service, local authorities shall indenture the services of snowmobilers, ice fishermen and Tonya Harding.

That any ice fisherman who leaves his shanty in any navigable canal, channel or waterway into the season of "liquid ice," shall be required to take residence in said shanty until the next ice fishing season.

Every weather forecaster (professional, amateur or those strictly for "entertainment value") will be encouraged to bring about spring temperatures in the following manner:

He, she or it will be provided a Ford Pinto and forced to drive on a rush hour freeway at speeds that match the high temperatures they forecast. As an example, if his forecast calls for balmy temps in the 60s and 70s, he should have no problem at least keeping out of the way of traffic. On the other hand, should he call for temperatures below freezing, his life will become more complicated and possibly shorter. Should he be brash enough to forecast sub-zero temperatures, he has to drive that speed, backwards.

To speed the seasonal placement of navigational aids and channel markers, those that use the water for non-boating purposes and are accustomed to working together as a team (Gee, hockey players come to mind!) will be required to remove said navigational aids at the end of the season and store them in their homes. If each and every one of them were to take responsibility for just one buoy, they should have them all back on station without difficulty by April 2nd every year.

Also by April 2nd of every year, the final snow bank removal shall have taken place. (It seems there is always at least one persistent snow bank left in the boat yard that refuses to melt. It's usually right underneath my outdrives.) Small children with sleds seem best suited to this task and should the chore be in danger of lingering on for lack of sled power, cross-country skiers should be at the ready to assist in a timely removal.

Be it understood that we are not trying to be unreasonable nor less than cooperative. But there comes a time to try all Cruiser's souls when one must say, "Enough is enough, let the boating begin!"

Signed this 1st day of April, 1995.

The Fine Art of Docking

When I first took up pleasure boating, the most complicated aspect for me was that docking part. You know, anybody can back it out, run it around the lake a few times, and most of us can even find our way back to our own section of the shore. But when you get close to the dock, those last few boat lengths, the final approach, when all the eyes in the marina are on you...for me, that was the tough part.

I know I'm not alone. I have several friends at work who are into boating and hey, a few drinks at the company picnic and it can turn into true confessions time. One individual once told me that he used to hang out in the shallows just outside the marina entrance, and fish until sunset. His eyes would comfortably adjust to the fading light and he would then enter the marina and attempt his docking maneuver. Docking in the dark made him feel safe from prying eyes and critical glances. He avoided public scrutiny for quite some time with this method until his wife embarrassed him back into the daylight with such remarks as "the vampire has landed."

Speaking of wives, that reminds me of another ploy. If you aren't very good at docking and you find it necessary to dock in the daylight in a reasonably populated marina, you can always send your wife out to the bow just before the crucial moment. It is even more advantageous to arm her with

Stupid Boat Tricks

an eye catching piece of boating equipment such as a brightly colored fender or shiny new boat hook. This way, her actions will distract the crowd from your own ineptitude and just to play it safe, you can even yell and scream at her from the safety of the cockpit and later blame the failure of the docking act on her misguided intervention. I used to have a friend who used to have a wife who used to put up with that. One word of advice, don't attempt this on vessels where the distance between the helm and the bow is shorter than the length of the boat hook.

Another creative docking concept is to "play possum." This is a technique a friend of mine would use on only those extreme occasions when the situation was hopeless and far too much pride was at stake. Pulling into a crowded resort harbor was generally such an occasion. The dockslingers would be yelling at him to park it over there...somewhere, and he knew this would mean rafting off, if he could indeed understand where it was they wanted him at all.

In this situation, my friend would "play possum" by getting close at a dead-slow speed, then killing the engine and faking mechanical failure. He did this every year at Put-In-Bay during Regatta week, until they caught on to him. He told me you'd be surprised how angry people will get with you when you're under power and start looking confused. But kill that engine and start throwing docklines at them and they become "heroes" who will deftly warp you into your space and even secure your lines for you while you "recover" from the dizzy spell caused by your near tragedy. If you want, you can save some face here by quickly entering the engine compartment and instantly diagnosing the cause of the "failure." Score extra points if you can blame it on someone else...maybe that woman with the boat hook.

But my favorite docking maneuver has to be the one I learned from Ken Miller. I have to admit, it's not his own method, but one a friend of his has successfully used for years. All it takes is a calm, cool attitude and the silent knowledge of your own lack of skill. Here's what he did:

Whenever he was approaching the marina and he didn't want to risk the docking himself for whatever reason, perhaps the day was windy or the dock was crowded, he would decide it was time for "a docking lesson." He'd turn the helm over to just about anyone, wife, kids, even guests. Then he'd go out to the bow with a dock line. And as the novice bumped and squeaked around the pilings, he'd just stand out there on the deck, look at the first person he could find, smile, shrug his shoulders and throw them the dockline. To this day, he is considered a generous man of incredible patience, and eventually, one of those kids finally did learn how to dock that darn boat.

The point here is that if you think their motivations and silly behaviors are unnecessary, perhaps we can all take our own insecurities and lack of certain experiences less to heart. It's pleasure boating, it's for fun, and remember: docking is an art…be you da Vinci, Picasso or Jackson Pollack.

Winter Cruising? a Letter for the Men

I know. You've probably just settled down on the sofa in your family room, it's almost kick-off time and you've just popped a fresh beer. Close at hand you've stacked all the newly arrived boat catalogs filled with all the toys and goodies a well-behaved boater deserves.

Outside the temperature is in the 20s (if your lucky), your kid is shoveling your sidewalk (in your dreams), and somewhere out there, it's snowing on your boat. Snow...snow is water waiting to become a lake.

If this day goes well, the home team won't be too badly embarrassed, the nautical accessory you lust for most will be on sale, and soon you will be asleep...dreaming of warm waters, new harbors and Great Lakes Summers yet to come. Is that all you have to do this winter? I'll bet your wife's plans are different. And if you look too comfortable, I'll bet some of those plans will include you. You sir, are a Boat Potato!!

"Moi?" you ask. "A Boat Potato?"

Yes, one who ceases to function during that brief period of time known as "winter Storage," is a Boat Potato. The first sign of the coming hibernation is the instinct to gather and pile printed material on things you usually do. And it can happen to anyone; man, woman, child, mascot, anyone! Come on! Just because the boat is up on blocks doesn't mean you have to get shrink wrapped too! This is the time of year for Winter Cruising!

Relax, Winter Cruising does not imply bundling up in arctic grade foul weather gear and battling your way out of a frozen channel to brave the wind-tossed, open regions of the lakes like some of those nuts around Chicago have been known to do. I may work on a boating magazine but I am not crazy!

To us, Winter Cruising means packing up the same luggage we use every weekend through the summer, with the same, comfortable, casual clothes we love so dearly (although we do leave the shorts at home and take an extra sweatshirt instead). Then, we throw them into the trunk of the land yacht (car) and shove off. Off to where? Why, off up the coast to some waterfront village that desperately needs discovering. Perhaps somewhere we've never been before. You would be surprised at how many of the ports and villages we boaters visit in the summer, are right there in the very same place all winter long! And they're open too!

Traveling by Land Yacht can be great. If you're a sailor, you'll be amazed at how fast your land yacht can travel. Some do 50, 60 miles an hour! And if you're a power boater, you'll be stunned by the fuel economy…why, you could probably save enough to stay at some quaint Bed & Breakfast for the whole weekend and if you haven't figured it out yet, you probably have a crew member who'd like to come a long.

Seriously, winter is the perfect time to "check out" some new harbor or yacht basin you have considered putting on your cruising plans for "someday." You can visit the harbor, get a good visual on the approach, look for recognizable landmarks that aren't on the charts, scout out the shops and local attractions, even enjoy a nice quiet dinner in an uncrowded waterfront restaurant! We make such a trip about once a month in the "cooler" season.

Stupid Boat Tricks

Think about it, traveling to picturesque waterfront locations for the pure beauty and pleasure of it all is exactly what *Great Lakes Cruiser* is all about. So what's the difference? Four or five times a year you make the trip by Chrysler instead of Chris Craft, by S-10 rather than 8-2. It will give you the opportunity to discover something few other boaters ever know: The beauty and the serenity that befalls these Great Lakes in the Winter. I think you'll find that a good Winter Cruise is the best way to peel a Boat Potato...

What's under the Tarp?

It's spring, that delightful time of year to once again play: "What's Under The Tarp?" I know, it sounds like a bad game show and would probably draw low ratings. But given time, truth and honesty, and the American way, I'm certain it could be far more socially relevant programming than what is currently offered during the daytime hours. This is a game I enjoy every spring, mostly because I'm so good at it. In fact, I am known as the "Columbo" of my marina, a status I have worked hard to attain. Here's how the game is played:

Every spring, we all venture out to the marina to untarp our vessels. At least, a "vessel" is what we left under there last fall. Now, it may very well be a treasure trove of forgotten items and hard to identify remains. I started to hone my legendary skills while working on my own craft, Moonraker, several seasons ago. Deep within the dusty hulk of my vessel, there in the still stagnant light, I came across two items of special interest.

The first was a small square object, originally black now covered with a fine white powder and trimmed with a fuzzy green and copper colored growth. The other was a short, cylindrical object, colored dark tan and black, about a half inch in diameter and perhaps two inches long. While hard as a rock, it weighed virtually nothing and my first reaction was that it was part of some high-tech equipment made from some futuristic alloy.., perhaps left there by space aliens known to hide in unoccupied boats during the off-season.

I carefully conveyed these objects back to the surface and set them out on the picnic table so that I could examine them in the bright sunlight. Just then, one of my marina mates from down the pier happened along and observed my investigation.

"Good Lord, what is that stuff!?" he exclaimed in disbelief.

"This," I held up the small square object with the white powder and the green growth, "is my beeper. It turned up missing last fall and I had mistakenly assumed I had lost it in the car or in the parking lot at work. Observe the white powder and the flowery growth. Left in the on position all winter, the batteries have long since expired and erupted in a corrosive flow that ended the useful life of this unit...probably around November sometime."

"Amazing!" he exclaimed. "I would never have recognized it! And what's that?" He pointed at the short, cylindrical object.

"That, is the petrified remains of a partially eaten Labor Day hot dog, obviously abandoned in a convenient hiding place by the child of a guest who desired other culinary experiences. Note the alternating brown and black markings. This wiener was grilled and judging by its degree of shriveling, it was probably a Ball Park Frank."

"You have a real talent for this...maybe you can help me with these."

And with that, he produced a number of small objects himself from his trash bag and set them on the picnic table next to my own.

"This..." I picked up object number one, a rather formless tube-shaped thing, about ten inches long. It's exterior looked like it once had a translucent, mirror-like finish.

Now, it was corroded into a dirty silver and through the finish, you could see a molten mass of yellow-green mud inside. "...is a package of Ritz crackers. This package obviously fell from the box under your settee last fall and has spent the winter absorbing moisture near your bilge. Note the puncture in the wrapper. It obviously snagged something as it rolled to a low point in your hull...Next!"

"How astute!" he exclaimed as he set forth his next mysterious object.

It was a short, blackened cylinder about two inches high. Its shape was warped and flaws could be seen in its once-perfect exterior.

"A D-cell flashlight battery. This unit has spent the winter submerged in the bilge where it first shorted, then burst open. You obviously have a good amount of engine oil in your bilge. I'd check that. Also check your bilge pump as it has now spent the winter marinating in battery acid...Ray-O-Vac, I think."

"Astounding!" he shouted.

And so my afternoon went. From time to time, a fellow marina resident would interrupt my work to ask me to identify that quizzical object they had discovered below. And so it has continued over the years. There is only one man who ever challenged my findings and objected to the conclusion. For him, it was not a question of my skill, but it was a case of his own strong desire for a different outcome.

Last spring, the young, aggressive yuppie from the end of the pier came down and presented me with a small, flat, rectangular object that was blackened beyond recognition and so tough, it defied examination. As I started to look it over, he nearly pleaded with me.

"Please tell me this is the modem card for my laptop computer! I lost it last fall and wondering what happened to it has been driving me crazy all winter!"

"Where did you find this thing?"

"On a ledge down in my engine compartment...behind the fire extinguisher. It's my lost modem, isn't it!"
"Sorry," I said, "It's a Pop-Tart."
"A Pop-Tart?! No! It's got to be my modem!"
"Just a Pop-Tart...strawberry, vanilla icing."
"But what about my modem?"
"Your modem sleeps elsewhere..."
"This has to be it!"
"Think...Have you ever used your laptop down in the engine compartment?"
"No..."
"You've never surfed the web or faxed away for new spark plugs while huddling down there in the dark?"
"Don't be ridiculous."
"Then, how could this be your modem?"

And with that piece of logic, he wandered on down the pier, closely examining his new-found snack food along the way.

I am eternally thankful he didn't raise the obvious question: Just who would be eating those Pop-Tarts below the decks, anyway? But by the same token, the fact that he didn't ask has kept me from accepting his many barbecue invitations.

J.K.'s Law

You will find this boat trick incredibly stupid. So incredibly stupid, that we have had to greatly alter the names and identifying circumstances to protect ourselves from an even stupider law suit. This is also a bonus stupid boat trick, because not only de we bring you one mental midget of the marshlands, we bring you two! Yes, it's two for one month here at Stupid Boat Tricks, my holiday gift to you...

It was a warm, summer afternoon, when the young boater and his girlfriend pointed their 27-foot express cruiser out of the harbor and into the open lake. They were off on a weekend of fun and frolic at one of the Great Lakes' prime destinations. With the charting and plotting all done in advance, our captain, let's call him "Captain Lucky" for reasons that will soon become obvious, felt he had things well under control.

However, in just thirty minutes, he would make the most momentous decision of the weekend. That's how long it took to get away from the crowd of coastal boats and well-offshore. By this time, the girlfriend decided she just couldn't get enough of the studly Captain Lucky, what with skippering his own luxurious boat and all, and suggested they spend some quality time together down in the cabin. But Captain Lucky had a schedule to keep and rather than stop the boat and drift during this unscheduled break, he decid-

Stupid Boat Tricks

ed to use the autopilot...Yes, with the inevitable unknown before him, he set the autopilot, left the helm at full throttle and retired to the distractions of the cabin. (Well, there was no one near him as far as he could see, so why not, right?) I don't think there's one of you out there that would question my calling this (in my opinion) an act of incredible stupidity.

But this is where J.K.'s Law comes into effect. Just like Newton and Murphy, I have a list of laws that govern the area of my expertise. Number three on the hit parade states: "If there is more than one, complete, blithering idiot on the lake, they shall find each other." Enter Joe Fisherman.

Joe Fisherman had been trolling in a small boat quite some distance ahead of Captain Lucky. But Captain Lucky was detained in the cabin far longer than he had anticipated. They were now approaching each other on a collision course.

Unfortunately, Joe Fisherman had learned everything he needed to know about boating from his Uncle Bob, who hadn't taken a safe boating course either. Let's say there were some holes in the finer points of his education. One of them being the rules of the road concerning the right of way.

Joe Fisherman was crossing Captain Lucky's course, from left to right, meaning that Joe Fisherman had to give way to Captain Lucky. But Joe Fisherman was under the mistaken impression that because he was fishing he had the right of way.

Sorry, Joe. Read your regulations. According to the class I help teach for the U.S. Power Squadron, a FISHING boat has the right of way. The definition of a fishing boat refers to nets, trawls and stakes that need to be laid down and recovered on a set course. These boats have the right of way. Specifically, the rules state that "this does not include a vessel fishing with trolling lines or other fishing gear that does not restrict maneuverability." It seems the rules conclude that a commercial fishing vessel is FISHING. Two guys with a twelve pack and a couple of planer boards aren't FISHING, they're FISHIN'...and there's a very big legal difference.

But armed with a faulty knowledge that he had the unrevokable, deity-given, right of way, Joe Fisherman trolled on into the path of the bigger boat. He could see there was no one at the helm, but he proceeded to shout and wave his arms anyway. (Apparently Uncle Bob had also told him you don't need a horn as he didn't have one of those either.) The boats got closer. Joe Fisherman waved and shouted. Captain Lucky...continued to be detained.

It seems Uncle Bob also never explained about The General Prudential Rule, or The Rule of Good Seamanship, you know the one that says it's OK to break the rules in order to avoid a collision. Traffic school veterans will remember this as the "last clear chance to avoid the accident." Joe Fisherman literally waved his position on these rules. In fact, he yelled and waved right up to the moment of impact.

Both boats were extremely damaged, but did not sink. Both captains were extremely shook up, but miraculously, no one was hurt. J.K.'s Law #9: God watches over those too foolish to do so for themselves...in his spare time. (You can't always count on this.)

The authorities were summoned. A gaggle of pleasure boats gathered and offered assistance. An argument began over who got into whose way. Two tickets were issued, one to each skipper. One for failure to yield the right of way, and the other for failure to "keep a proper lookout." Both captains decided to fight their tickets...and lost. I know as a fact that Captain Lucky pleaded for assistance to fight this ticket from his insurance company. This too, was not a smart move. The lady on the phone said: "You were where when the accident happened?" The claim was paid, but then the policy was abruptly canceled, leaving our skipper to seek insurance elsewhere, where the rates are higher. Captain Lucky ain't so lucky anymore....

Wild Bill Hiccup and the T-Bone

A long time ago, on a Great Lake far away, there lived a sailor named Bill. Bill lived on the edge of things. He was what we would call today...extreme. He lived hard and played hard. He wasn't happy unless he was, as he put it, "Traveling at the speed of life." When he sailed, he always had the rail in the water, the spray in the face and "Top Gun" blaring from the stereo.

Bill also partied hardy and consumed more than his fair share of substances, both controlled and illicit. Hence the nick name, Wild Bill Hiccup. He and his friends would come out to the marina in the evenings, consume, inhale, imbibe and do whatever else they did, and then, well after dark, they'd go out on the lake in Wild Bill's 35-foot, racing-rigged, sailboat. To them, there was nothing like a healed-over, rail-in-the-water, thrill ride on a moonless night with the sails as tight as the crew and spray as sharp as they thought they were.

Being a safety-conscious, out-of-control, party animal, Wild Bill Hiccup never left the dock much before 10 P.M. after everyone else had come in. He never returned much later than 4 A.M., before the early fisherman ventured out. And he always preferred weeknights to weekends. He always said, this cut down on traffic that might get in his way and slow him down. Little did he know...

Stupid Boat Tricks

One hot summer night, when the moon was exceptionally dark and the crew were all exceptionally tight, they set sail for the open waters and the "high times" that awaited them. There they were, heeled-over into the pounding waves, with the spray on the deck, the stereo blaring and the hull carving along at record speed.

Suddenly, someone on deck realized that the great abundance of stars that are visible on moonless nights, were no longer visible before them. In fact, there was a great, black void before them. The entire crew, except for the heavy metal guys on the stereo, fell silent in bewilderment...what was eating up the stars?

Their bewilderment was abruptly ended by a large crash, as the sailboat came to a sudden stop. Crew members were thrown to the deck, everything in the cabin found the floor and the heavy metal guys on the stereo were knocked out of their groove and fell silent. It took a few seconds to realize what had happened...they had T-boned a freighter! Dead nuts center, at perfect right angles, at full speed, they had rammed a freighter out on the open lake.

What happened next was even more unbelievable. Most boats that commit this navigational faux paus, will often shatter their hull, or at least break-off that pointy end of the boat they used as a ramrod. These boats quickly drink the lake and go down, under the freighter, where they, and their crews, come out through the propellers Vegimatic style. But not this time. One of J.K.'s rules was in effect that night, the one that says "God watches over those too foolish to do so for themselves...in his spare time."

It seems two seasons before, Wild Bill had installed an unusually large, stainless steel bow pulpit on the boat...one that well-overhung the end of the bow and reached out into space in large, hooped shapes. It was this bow pulpit that had hit the freighter, and while it was mangled, it had worked like a giant spring. They had literally bounced off the freighter like a dud torpedo! And as they sat there in amazement that no one was hurt, that they weren't sinking, that no one was going to get washed through the huge props, God spoke directly to them in the form of a small, Oriental man: Down from the darkness, somewhere on the deck of the big ship, came a faint voice with a thick accent letting them know: "You very rucky..."

Epilogue: In the seasons that followed, the Great Lakes suffered low water levels and Wild Bill Hiccup spent more time aground on sandbars than ramming freighters. Convinced that the water gods were sending him a message, Bill sold the boat and when last heard from, had taken up extreme snowmobiling. Have you noticed that lack of snow these past few winters?

"Annie, Forget the Gun..."

I don't know how funny this will be, but in my opinion, it sure qualifies as stupid! Let me go back, just less than a year ago, to a night when I was pulling guest speaker duties at a Chicago-area boating club. After dinner and after my talk, I was approached by a rather stern woman who introduced herself as "a former law enforcement officer," rather than by name. Did you ever meet one of those people whose very nature and manner of speaking tends to intimidate, to put you on the defensive? This describes her perfectly. During the conversation that followed, I felt very much like a hostile witness on the stand.

It seems she and her husband had been on a boating vacation to the Straits of Mackinac area and had decided to venture into Canadian waters. They had never crossed the border before, by land or sea, and quite frankly, they were unprepared and uninformed. Long story short, on their first morning in the North Channel, they were ticketed by a customs officer for not having reported-in on their arrival.

According to her, they came in late, the town was closed up and they couldn't see the customs phone because a truck had parked in front of it. She claimed that a dock boy had told her she could just call-in in the morning. There was a customs officer on the dock in the morning and she approached him about checking in. His response was to tell her to return to her vessel where he would ticket her for not properly reporting.

She was attempting, through congressional intervention and bureaucratic red tape, to get the ticket overturned and to get her money back. I knew her cause was futile and I could tell by the way she tried to twist and redefine everything I said, that the poor customs officer had probably ticketed her out of frustration. I would later hear another version of this story that would substantiate that theory. Some people go into a situation with a "how do I comply to the rules" attitude. Others seem to challenge the reason for the rules and try to make a case for why they should be allowed to do things their way. Some folks get ticketed, some don't. 'Nuff said.

Several weeks ago, this same woman called me at the office. She had indeed taken my advice and had convinced her husband to give those kind, Canadian people another try. In fact, they would be leaving in just a few days for the Bruce Peninsula! However...she was calling me as a last resort because she was not getting the answers she needed (more likely, the answers she wanted) concerning several Canadian laws. I consider myself a reasonable expert in that field and tried to help her.

She asked me about porta-potties Yes, they are illegal in Canada. They must all be converted to permanently-mounted marine heads with deck-top pumpout fittings, I told her.

"But Why?"

"Because, in the past, too many people have secretly dumped them over the side of the boat in the middle of the night."

"But I'm a former law enforcement officer, I would never do that!"

"I'm sure, but they don't know that."

"I could tell them, don't you think that should make a difference?"

Stupid Boat Tricks

"I'm sure you'd tell them, but no, it would make no difference, there are no exceptions to the law."

"But it seems like such a waste to do that for just one trip..."

As I tried to hang-up, she raised another topic.

"What's this about needing a U.S. government radio license for our VHF?"

"Yes, Canada is a foreign country. We have a reciprocal licensing agreement with them. Their licenses are good over here, and ours are good over there, but you have to have one."

"But we don't need one over here..."

"This is here, there is there. You have to have one and right now, there is no way you have time to get one before your trip."

"Well, I'll just leave the microphone at home then, and I think you'll agree that they can't ticket me for that!"

"No, I won't agree with anything. I strongly suggest you get a license before you enter Canadian waters!"

"Well," (she changed the topic) "I've got one more question for you. What would be the problem of me carrying a loaded shotgun below decks?"

"What!?!?" I was in shock.

"A loaded shotgun, I never travel without one!"

"Ma'am, I would strongly encourage against doing that!"

She got defensive. "My NRA pamphlet says I can take long arms including shotguns and rifles into Canada!"

"Yes, you can," I began to explain. "It's handguns that are illegal, but my wife's late grandfather was a world-champion skeet and trap shooter as well as an avid hunter. He did this all the time. To take firearms across the border, you must meet face to face with a customs official, there is a mountain of paper work and you can plan on an hour in the booth with the customs guys and that's if they like you!

Also, you have to have a reason for bringing them in...a scheduled competition, hunting season, and you're hunting had better be in season and you should already have your license! They just don't let you bring them in because they make you feel warm and fuzzy."

"But you need something like this when you travel these days!" she insisted.

"Ma'am, I can't think of one reason why you would need to boat with a loaded shotgun in the Great Lakes."

"Drug dealers! They'll steal your boat and kill you to use your boat to smuggle drugs!"

"That's in the Caribbean, ma'am. I have never heard of one case of that happening here. The Great Lakes are a rather closed system and there're not many places to run."

"Well, what about illegal alien smugglers? You covered that in your own magazine."

"They would prefer to not be seen by you and be as unnoticed as possible. They aren't going to hijack your boat and use it for evil purposes."

"Then what about those ruffians they've written about in Milwaukee Harbor? You can't deny that they are out of line and harassing innocent people!"

"That's still no justification to aim a shotgun at them, ma'am. As a former law enforcement officer, you should know that. I'll say it again, in the Great Lakes, there is no reason at all to carry a firearm of any kind when you're pleasure boating!"

She didn't agree with me, as I am sure she didn't agree with the other people she had tried to convince that there was a loophole for her somewhere. Again, I advised her not to go to Canada, and I think I asked her politely to not enter Lake Huron or Lake St. Clair, either.

I hope you take warning in this story that there are indeed, people out there who, in the spirit of confrontation, might pull a weapon on you. There is no need to carry one

Stupid Boat Tricks

of your own. This is not Dodge City, it's the Great Lakes. Just be calm, be cool, back away, surrender the right of way and anything else the gunman wants, don't challenge, and when you're clear, call the local authorities. Hey, you're not going to get mugged on the water, most muggers can't afford boats!

But wait, this little tale isn't over! Just last week, I received a call from a friend of mine in the OPP, let's call her "informed, reliable source." Informed, reliable source told me that the night before, they had indeed arrested an Indiana couple in a harbor on the Bruce Peninsula. There were several charges they would probably plea-bargain but the woman's demands and challenges left them no other option.

It started with a young man in a zoom boat cutting them off, to which she responded with an obscene radio transmission…right in front of an OPP boat. Upon boarding, they discovered she had no FCC license or restricted operator's permit. Further searching found she had a non-converted chemical toilet on board. And there, next to the toilet, was a loaded, 12-gauge pump-action shotgun. Hmmmm.

Well, they started writing and she started challenging and eventually, she wound up in cuffs and inspecting the interior of an OPP "welcome centre." Oddly, of all the things she said, one of her demands was to talk to me!

"Did I know her and did I want to talk to her?" asked the informed, reliable source.

"Not with a ten-foot shotgun," I said, or is that, not without one?

Babes in Toyland

Well, the boat is tarped and the barrage has started. Not the barrage of snow drifts and ice storms, those will begin soon enough. The barrage I'm talking about is the one of catalogs and sale papers filled with every boater's dreamscape of gadgets, gizmos and geegaws.

It's amazing how those boat supply places know when we've put our boats away for the winter, and what's even more amazing is what they expect from us: They think we have nothing better to do between now and Christmas, but sit around and drool over all the electronic toys in their catalogs! (The ones I get this time of year are mostly electronics, aren't yours?)

Sometimes I think our whole boating community has gone electronically crazy. I mean, can't we enjoy the simplicity, the quiet, rustic serenity that the water has always been without a menagerie' of battery powered transmitters, receivers, detectors, sensors and indicators?

It really hit me this summer when I watched Jenvey refit his boat after his bout with the bolt. There were all kinds of empty electronics boxes in our dumpster and every time they'd come along and empty it, he'd fill it up again. TVs, stereos, VCRs, digital doohickies and graphical gizmos...He even has ham radio stuff on his boat! He comes out here to get away from the rest of the world, and then wants to talk

Stupid Boat Tricks

to everyone in it. Even Ken Miller, the purist, asked me if I thought a TV like Jenvey's would fit on top of his hanging locker...Amazing.

But what's even more amazing is the guy down the pier. This guy's boat looks like he drove it through the javelin tryouts. I mean there's white poles sticking up all over! He's got radar, GPS, Loran, auto pilot, depth sounders, fish finders and more, along with extra read outs and back up systems. If his batteries die, they'd have to put the boat on a ventilator. And you know what? He never leaves the bay! He goes out, two or three hours at a time, and comes back. He never spends the night on his boat. Probably not enough room on board what with all those electronics.

And here's another strange thing: He'll sit at his dock for hours...running his radar. Like a fog might roll in and he'll get lost on his way to the bathroom. You can see it up there, spinning around. Of course I can tell whenever he's running it because it interferes with my own...my...our...well OK, it rips the crap out of my TV! There, I said it! His radar beacon is just too close and too much for my own amplified TV antenna system and the front end circuit for my color TV. He doesn't interfere when I watch a video, just the live broadcast stuff.

In my embarrassment here, I am reminded of an argument my children had in the back seat of the family car this past summer:

"Did so!"
"Did not!"
"Did so!"
"Did not!" (progressive negotiation runs in my family)
"Did so!"
"Dad, Columbus didn't have GPS when he discovered America, right?"
"Dad, He had to! Loran don't go out that far!"

I guess the moral here is that there are no more hardcore, sail-by-the-stars, purists. Just as there are no more coonskin capped wilderness men. Just as there are no more quill-and-ink, first-draft authors. And I'm sure if the Shakespeares, the Crocketts and the Columbuses of yesteryear were around today, they too would revel in the advantages of word processors, night-vision scopes and navigation computers. There is no need to toe a hard line to keep things primitive when a reasonably affordable accessory could make things more comfortable.

Your boat should be your cottage, your escape pod, your home away from home. It's not a trial or tribulation to have survived (those are your trips, not your boat). Boating is after all, a hobby. And your boat is a very serious and sophisticated...toy. So when the new toy catalogues come in this fall, look, dream, plan, drool...and then pray to Santa that you've been a good boy or girl. Personally, I'm dreaming of a new multi-scanning VHF this year, just like Jenvey's.

When in Rome...

Recently, friends of ours returned from Italy, specifically Rome. It's warmer there this time of year than it is here, a fact they reminded us of several times. And as we sat around the living room looking at roll after roll of color prints just back from the drug store...it hit me. It hit me while looking at a picture of a large thumb standing next to the Colosseum and then again when leafing through The Visitor's Memory Book starring the same famous piece of architecture. (Thank God it was in Italian and didn't require reading then and there!)

What hit me? Follow along:

The Romans were the most technically and socially advanced people of their time. Yet they fought their battles with pointed sticks and rudimentary shields while wearing mini skirts. I mean, today, we could beat those guys, right? Exactly! But they built this sports arena called the Colosseum. It took me some time to convince my son that they didn't name it after the one in LA.

Now, this sports arena was quite a place. Gladiators and other combatants would fight there for the amusement of the crowd. From time to time, they would even flood the place and put on live sea battles! Amazing! To me, this was a vindication that my favorite pastime is indeed superior to those of the winter months. You never hear of the Romans packing the place with the fluffy white stuff and staging snowball fights or skiing exhibitions. I have often said that snow is water waiting to become a lake. Obviously the Romans agreed.

But let's get back to the matter at hand. If the Romans, with their bronze age technology and limited tools can flood the Colosseum at will and float boats around in there...think what a twentieth century, technowizard backed by the power of Black & Decker could do!

That's it people! There is no longer any reason to go boatless for several months during the year. Simply flood your basement! Heck, half the basements I've had didn't need much help in flooding at all. In fact, we struggled to get the water out. Just think how easy it would be to keep the water in! And there's water everywhere you look down there. Any pipe will do!

I figure two or three feet would be enough. You don't need to float the big boat. But you could have a lot of fun with the dingy, the swim fins and maybe the radio controlled boat where you could practice docking and other maneuvers. Personally I plan to stir up the water a little with the washing machine and get some time in with heavy weather conditions too. And here's another possibi...

[I'm sorry, but due to circumstances beyond my control, I have been asked not to finish this article and to give up all nautical plans for the basement. If I continue, I have been promised not only a change of address, but an alteration in the state of the physical being...But as a consolation, I know there's not even a chance of encountering a snowball there!]

Part of an Old, Dead Bird...

This is less of a stupid boat trick and more of a stupid boater's trick, but it's still an amusing tale and yes, one that happened to me. While I am not particularly proud of my actions, there is a devious boy inside me that would do this again if the opportunity presented itself.

It was going to be a unique vacation. We, (my wife, two kids and small dog), were going to head into the northern reaches of the lakes aboard our Sea Ray 30, Moonraker. We would spend a week at the docks in a sleepy little community and share our days with my sister-in-law, her husband and two sons. They would be staying in a nearby cottage and have a car and together, we would do the sight-seeing thing. It would be the first time we had ever vacationed together and the two sisters were very excited about it.

To add to this fun, my nephews would have been staying at my wife's parents for the preceding two weeks not far from where we lived and wouldn't it be fun, thought my wife, if we were to bring them up to the cottage with us, on the boat. The other female involved also thought this would be great fun but I had reservations: I had often referred to these nephews as Terror 1 and Terror 2, with what I thought was good reason. They were rude, unruly, disrespectful little demons as "free spirited," pre-teen children often are. On top of this, they will have spent the last fourteen days in the hands of Spoil-Me-Grandma, the most notorious, over-indulgent grandparent in the Great Lakes. And the six of us and a small dog were going to spend several days on board a 30-foot fiberglass cave...

I knew I was in trouble when my in-laws came to drop off the nephews at the dock. My visibly wearied father-in-law merely shook my hand and said "Good luck." Grandma kissed, Wife smiled, Cousins watched nervously, Dog went below, and the two Terrors...cast evil grins at each other.

We were off, and the next two days and two nights were actually worse than I anticipated, my sanity preserved only by some rather creative thinking: When they didn't understand why they actually had to do as they were told, my wife convinced them "it was the law of the sea" and until we hit shore, the captain was in complete charge. Thanks, Wife...we pull into harbor every night! Why couldn't she say, "until the voyage is over..."

When unruly behavior found its way into the cabin at night, I suggested that if they didn't settle down, we would have to have an abandon ship drill in which we prove that life jackets can indeed be effectively worn as suppositories. My own children, wise to my ploy and equally tired of the Two Terrors, chimed in that not only was I serious, but that I had just bought new, extra-firm life jackets.

Things I used to own that now sleep at the bottom of Lake Michigan: one CD, my flare kit, my favorite BBQ spatula, the BBQ, one fishing rod, one stereo speaker cover formerly mounted on the radar arch (don't even ask), and the manuals to both my GPS and my depth sounder.

By the end of the third day, we were exhausted. We pulled into our
port of destination only to find out that my sister-in-law and her husband would not be arriving until the next morning...we had one more night to survive!

To placate the Terrors, dinner was at their favorite fast

food establishment right there at the marina. As they started to fight and shove between themselves at the table, I eyed the display of type-I life jackets in the boat store window across the driveway. But then, another idea hit me and I was in a moment of weakness...I looked at the younger one who was chomping away on his chicken nuggets.

"So," I asked him, "how's that old dead bird you're eating there?"

Everyone at the table stopped cold, everyone was in shock, especially the Terrors.

"Say, what, Uncle John?" came the voice from under the nuggets.

"I said, how's that old dead bird you're eating there?"

"What dead bird?"

"What do you think chicken nuggets are made of?"

"...chicken??"

"Well, a chicken's a bird and that one is certainly dead...and it's not a whole one...so...you're eating part of an old, dead bird."

There was silence, the child's jaw dropped. Then his brother, eating a cheeseburger, started to laugh.

"What are you laughing at?" I asked.

His eyes got big and he stopped chewing.

"You're eating part of a dead cow!"

My teen-aged daughter, not one to miss an opportunity, pulled a bacon strip from her own burger and said:

"And this is part of a dead pig!"

She then shoved it into her mouth and licked her lips with gusto. The Two Terrors looked at each other, they looked at their food, they looked at us and then back at their food again. Silence reigned. It had never occurred to them to question the source of their favorite food. They finished their meals, slowly, and seemed to take comfort knowing that the old dead potato probably didn't have a name.

That night there was peace and quiet on the boat and by

noon, Mom and Dad had shown up, checked into their cabin and the Two Terrors officially changed residences. However, the reason for their delay was that they had brought his mother along with them. The gentle old lady wanted to spend time with her grandsons and started off the visit by cooking them a large, home-style ham dinner.

The dinner hour was broken by a loud shriek. I didn't go investigate because deep inside, I knew. After dinner, my most perturbed sister-in-law showed up on the dock to let us know how upset her mother-in-law was. It seems that about halfway through dinner, one of the Terrors had piped up with: "Gee Grandma, you sure know how to cook an old, dead pig!" We have never vacationed with them again.

The Sins of Our Fathers...

It's March, and soon we will be pulling the tarps and splashing the hulls for another season. It seems appropriate now to tell you about something that happened to me last fall.

Like half our staff, I teach basic boating safety for my respective boating organization. And I have to tell you, sometimes you meet the strangest people in those beginner courses. Take Mr. X as an example:

He was in his early forties, very-well dressed, in fact, obviously over-dressed for boat class. I gave him the benefit of the doubt and assumed he had come to this evening's class right from his office. He was obviously a man of means in a powerful position.

However, Mr. X also had a very large chip on his shoulder. It was obvious from the scowl on his face, the way he sat in the chair and the opportunistic, "I'll teach you a thing or two myself" look in his eyes. Mr. X was also very short of stature. I put one and seven together and came up with one-hundred and forty three...he was a classic, napoleonic over-achiever.

My next clue came when I asked the class about their boats. You see, our boating group teaches our classes tag-team style, meaning I teach the same part of the course on different nights to every class we conduct. The students get a new instructor every week. This was my week to meet Mr.

X and I always start my talk with asking about what kind of boats the students have.

"How many people here have boats sixteen feet or less?" I asked the crowded auditorium. A number of hands went up. "Between sixteen and twenty-six?" About half the class raised their hands. "Between twenty-six and forty?" Again, a healthy number but much less the previous group raised their hands. In fact, by the end of this group, everybody in the room had raised their hands...except Mr. X. Since he had captured my attention when I first walked in and deemed him "one to keep an eye on," I had done just that. He had not yet raised his hand and he was sitting there, grinning with an "I dare you to go on" look in his eye, his hand at the ready. I gave in.

"Over forty feet?" I cautiously asked.

Bingo! His hand shot up like a rocket and he quickly looked around to make sure he was still in this category all by himself. Yes. He owned the biggest boat in class! I bit.

"Over forty feet! That's quite a boat!" I said politely. "Just how big is it?"

"Forty-five feet!" came his gleefully snarled reply.

"My!" I was genuinely taken aback. "Is this your first boat?"

This was my polite way of asking him what the owner of a forty-five-foot boat was doing in a class for raw recruits. Suddenly, his tone turned a little more explanatory.

"Well, my first boat but I've been doing this for years!"

"Crewing with a friend?"

"My dad, actually. He taught me everything I need to know. When I was a kid growing up, we took our boat everywhere!"

I smelled something. Why would a man who already knows everything he needs to know, be sitting here in my basic boat class? He has also told me something else: His boating experience with his father is not very recent. He didn't start off with "last summer" and work his was back to his childhood, he mentioned his childhood and left it at that. Being a glutton for punishment, and overly curious, I pressed on.

"Oh, then is this your dad's boat you've got now?"

"Oh no! I bought this baby brand new! This one's a little too big to trailer…"

The smugness of his last statement really started to fill in the blanks. Not only was his last boating experience some twenty or thirty years ago, but his dad's boat was trailerable, not a forty-plus footer.

"I see," I said, as convincingly as I could. "This class is a great place to brush up on the basics. A lot of boaters—"

"I don't need any brushing up!" He interrupted. "My dad was an expert at all this boating stuff and taught me everything."

Well, now I knew his dad was deceased too. I hoped he hadn't been killed in a boating accident but I was beginning to have my doubts. But above that, my own curiosity was getting to me. If he was convinced he knew it all, what was he doing here?

"Well, a certificate from a course like this can save you lots on your insurance." I must have hit a nerve for he fell silent for a few smoldering seconds and color came to his face.

"I told you, my dad taught me everything I need to know about this stuff!"

With that, the course chairman stepped up beside me and quietly handed me several pages with a cover letter and an envelope stapled to it. I quickly, and silently, skimmed the letter and the other pages. The rest of the class had no idea what I was reading but our forty-five-foot skipper did! He sat, there, red-faced, angry, but silent.

It was a most interesting letter from a judge of the local district court. It seems our dear Mr. X was in attendance by way of a court order. You know, the kind of court order they issue as part of a punishment instead of hard jail time.

According to my reading, it seems Mr. X had taken his forty-five footer out on the river and associated Great Lakes waters one sunny weekend last summer. During the course of his brief afternoon family jaunt, Mr. X had: 1. Run two other boats aground in the channel by failure to yield right of way. 2. Sped through a "no wake zone" at such speed as to endanger the anchored fishermen. 3. He briefly secured his boat to a navigational buoy in the river before breaking free and drifting into the path of converging freighters. (Repair bills to the buoy for some $600 were paid by Mr. X and attached to the document.) 4. Motored into a marked swimming area (so his kids could go swimming) and in the process, he ran aground near the shore. 5. He then called the Coast Guard for a tow on his unlicensed VHF radio (required at the time) and 6. Became abusive when the Coast Guard, the Harbor Patrol and the Sheriff's Department all converged on his motionless craft. 7. A breathalyzer test indicated he had been drinking but was below the level of legal intoxication.

Seeing as this was his first offense, or rather, first rampage of offenses, the judge went fairly easy on him. He would serve no jail time, but there were some hefty fines to pay and highlighted in the letter: Mr. X was to attend and graduate this course before again operating his vessel. In addition, he was to spend one-hundred hours of community service, working in this course as an assistant after his completion. Not only was Mr. X going to sit through this course now, but he was going to do so twice a year, for the next three years!

After quickly skimming the documents, I smiled and glanced up at Mr. X who was flushed with embarrassment and struggling to keep silent. There were many things I wanted to say but our goal is to educate, not to intimidate. I knew if I were insulting, all I would accomplish would be to close his mind even more. But I also needed to say something strong enough to break through that crusty exterior and let him know I was on to him.

"Your Dad taught you to do all this, did he?" I asked in my best, Monty Python voice. It worked. The tension broke with a contagious laughter that started in the back and soon overtook the entire room including Mr. X himself. And as he shook his head in answer to my question, I realized he would not be a problem the rest of the evening.

In fact, after that, I heard that Mr. X became much more cooperative in class, enjoyed the program and passed his final with flying colors. I guess the bottom line here is that we all can learn more about something we know everything about. When we think we know it all, that's when we become dangerous. Personally, I have taught this course twice a year for several seasons and every year, I learn something new from the very students I am supposed to be teaching.

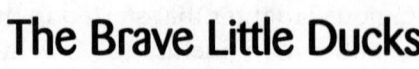

The Brave Little Ducks

Once upon a time, a long time ago, Chuck and Sue had their first little pocket cruiser on Lake St. Clair. It was a small, shallow draft sailboat with a swing keel and it even came complete with a trailer. Having their own trailer meant they weren't dependent on the marina operator's schedule. They could launch themselves! They could be the first ones in the water in the spring, and the last ones out in the fall...or maybe even early winter if they felt like it.

One cool, crisp autumn morning, they were out exercising this freedom along the northern shore of the lake. Their shallow draft let them go into the marshy areas around Bouvier Bay and Grassy Island, a real naturalist's haven this time of year with all the migrating birds and other animals

preparing for the coming winter.

Then, in the reeds along the north shore of Grassy Island, Sue spotted a family of ducks. Wanting a closer look, they cranked up the keel to "rowboat draft" and ghosted in silently under jib sail alone. They drew closer, but the ducks didn't take off in a panic.

"The must not see us," whispered Chuck.

"Maybe they see us, and just want the free meal," whispered Sue as she crept below for crackers and bread crumbs for their new little friends.

Ever so slowly, they drew closer, afraid that every ripple in the water, every movement of the sail, might cause the little duck family to leave without their bread crumbs.

"What brave little ducks!" Whispered Sue as they crept to within just a few feet of the shoreline. "They're just waiting for us to get there!"

To set things at ease, Sue decided to let their intentions be known to the ducks and she cast a few preliminary crumbs upon the water.

Now, with the ducks familiar with marina life in our end of the lake, this would have normally started a free-for-all, but these late-season ducks just wouldn't move. They just sat there, waiting for Chuck and Sue to come right in among them.

"Maybe they're too afraid to leave the reeds this time of year—" whispered Chuck, but he never finished the sentence.

He was interrupted by a terrible "thump" that broke the quiet, morning air...They had rammed one of the ducks! In a panic, Sue leaned over the side of the small sailboat and shrieked in horror as a now headless duck drifted past the cockpit.

Suddenly, their attention was stolen by the calamity taking place less than a boat length away, on the shore. A man, dressed in camouflage, rose up from the reeds and with a face as red and as twitching as the trigger finger on the large shotgun he carried, he managed to spit out the words:

"Those are decoys, you idiot!"

Quick-thinking Sue, remembering that one of the first rules of safe boating is to never antagonize men with firearms, immediately spoke up.

"And fine decoys they are too! You must be so proud!"

It worked. The red drained from the man's face and he relaxed his grip on the trigger. Even a slight smile crept into one corner of his mouth. And as Chuck spun the boat around and pull-started the three horse Mercury, they could hear him reply as they puttered away:

"Oh, really? I make them myself…"

Do Not Read 'til All Hallow's Eve...

Keeping with the tradition of our Halloween issue, I have a tale for you that is so scary, so frightening, I have waited until the end of the boating season to share it with you. I fear that if you were to read this during your time of cruising on the lakes, you might become so frightened as to return home and never venture upon these seas again.

There is an evil force upon these lakes, that befalls cruising pleasure boaters late in the day. I have witnessed this foul curse all over the lakes this summer. What evil force do I speak of? I don't know. It has no name. But it appears to befall boaters within the last mile or two of their daily voyages before entering the harbor. It creates an anomaly in the time-space continuum and can actually distort and alter the dimensions of their boat, although only temporarily! Some say it travels on an ill-wind. Some say it comes up from the depths. Sometimes, it has been known to travel in small, aluminum cans in the cooler.

Gasp! What? Yea, it is true...My first indication that this force was loose among us came over the VHF radio. On many occasions this season, I sat in transient harbors and heard vessels requesting dockage for the night. I heard 23-foot sailboats that had reportedly developed 9-foot keels out there in the darkness. This made it necessary for them to be assigned slips normally reserved for the 40-, 50- and 60-foot boats. But of course, since most harbors charge by the linear foot for dockage, these terribly distorted boats were not penalized for the curse of their excessive draft. They got the 60-foot dock and only had to pay for 23 feet of it.

Miraculously, by morning, the curse was gone and the these same, 9-foot draft, 23-footers would slip out of the harbor's shallow entrance through a mere three feet of water! Frightening, isn't it? At first, I sighed in relief that this evil force only seemed to affect sailboat keels, and myself being a powerboater, well, I was safe.

But then the evil force hit closer to home! One afternoon on the radio, I heard a 24-foot powerboat approaching the harbor requesting dockage to accommodate his horrific, 18-foot beam! My God...the evil force had made his boat almost square! Again, he would need to be docked in the big-boat slips (but at the 24-foot rate) until the spell had passed. Fortunately, by morning, this boat with the 18-foot beam was able to be towed away on an 8-foot wide trailer by a down-sized sport utility vehicle.

I was then convinced that the force could attack either power or sailboats, but only smaller vessels, distorting their odd dimension...draft or beam. But then I found reason to believe that these alleged smaller vessels were actually much larger vessels that had been shrunk by the evil force! Upon what do I base this conclusion? Several times I encountered these less-than 25-foot vessels that had been granted 50 plus-foot docks and when the local harbormaster tried to put two such vessels in the same slip, he met with irate skippers (obviously possessed) who screamed their protests that they indeed needed these huge wells all to themselves! Why would they make such a ridiculous statement if they didn't indeed know that once the evil spell had passed, their twenty-some foot boats with the deep drafts or wide beams would again grow to be the 50-footers they had been before the spell had caught them? Having two such

Stupid Boat Tricks

collapsible boats on the same dock could be disastrous.

But then, things really got scary...As the summer progressed, I saw the evil force affecting boat lengths as they moved between the gas docks and the transient slips! On more than one occasion I heard 30-foot powerboats, much like my own, requesting dockage for the night via VHF. At the gas docks, these boats registered as thirty-footers. But somewhere coming down the canals, this evil force grasped their poor vessels and swelled their length considerably! Right there in the marina in front of witnesses! The worst was the poor owner of one such 30-footer that tried with all effort to fit into his 30-foot assigned slip...only to realize he had miraculously grown to nicely over 40-feet! He had even grown graphics on his hull to confirm his new-found length! It was only after a heated discussion with the harbormaster that the poor boat owner agreed to pay for the erroneous extra footage and, at least for the night, be the craft he had grown to be.

Frightening, isn't it that this could happen to the boat sharing the slip right next to you. It's frightening that some vessels are forced to anchor-out without access to facilities because the bigger slips are all filled with demonically possessed skippers, waiting for their boats to grow. Here's some more scary stuff: Imagine coming in during bad weather or maybe you're shorthanded...and there's no dockhand to help you. Maybe you've had to wait a long time at the gas dock because there's just not enough people around the marina to get to you right away.

Where is that extra dockhand? He disappeared too, because of budget cuts and dropping revenue. Think about it. One of these shrinking boats comes in and the harbormaster is out ten or fifteen bucks. If, during the height of the season, just one boat a day does this, that's enough money to pay a dockhand that could have been there. That's scary!

What can you do about it? Unfortunately, statistics show

that if you're reading this magazine, the evil force tends to leave your boat alone. It's those other boaters out there not protected by a subscription to GLC that tend be the problem. All too often, in these showdowns on the dock, the harbormaster stands alone. Stand with him, even if you stand on the safety of your own boat. Just stand up and be visible with your hands in your pockets. There is no need to get involved, just watch. With three, four, or a dozen of you just watching, you can miraculously lift the evil spell and return all these afflicted boats to their proper dimensions and bring peace to the harbor.

With Apologies…

'Twas the night before Christmas, and all down the pier,
Not a creature was stirring, for no one was near.

The boats were all tarped and protected from freeze,
Awaiting the water and a warm summer breeze.

The children were cranky and aching our heads,
So a long time ago, we had sent them to bed.

So with Maw in her joggers, and I in my vest,
We had just settled down for a well deserved rest.

When down from the boathouse, there arose such a clatter,
I sprang from the bed to see what was the matter.

From there in the window, I could take in the sights,
To see what had triggered the security lights.

The moon on the crest of the snow that was there,
Had lit the marina like a parachute flare.

When what to my wondrous eyes should arise,
But a miniature Chris Craft with eight tiny outdrives.

With a little old skipper so lively and quick,

John Kenneth Bruce

I knew in a moment it must be "Cap' Nick."

More rapid than jet skis his coursers they came,
And he laid on the air horn and called them by name.

Now Cobra, now Chevy, now Johnson and Mercury,
On Crusader, on Mopar, on Volvo and OMC.

To the top of the hoist, to the top of the wall,
He pushed down his throttles and gave it his all.

As dry leaves that before the wild hurricane fly,
When they meet with an obstacle, mount to the sky.

So up on the boathouse, his coursers they flew,
With a hold full of goodies and Cap' Nicholas too.

I ran down the stairs and out through the yard,
And opened the gate with my security card.

There in the isles of slumbering craft,
I encountered Cap' Nicholas, caught in the act.

He was dressed all in Gortex, from his head to his feet,
With a Sou'wester rain hat and a bright PFD.

A bundle of toys he had flung on his back,
And he looked like a fence just opening his pack.

He spoke not a word but went straight to his work,
And stuffed all the boat tarps for all they were worth.

There were Radars and Sat Nays, and marine VHFs,
Hand Helds and hailers and sounders for depths.

Stupid Boat Tricks

But when it came time, for my own humble craft,
An outdated Loran he pulled from his sack.

Then sticking a finger inside of his nose,
He gave me a wink and up the fly bridge he rose.

To the top of the decks, to the top of the masts,
He jumped in his Chris Craft and got away fast.

But I heard him exclaim as he coursed towards the west,
"Had you not been so nasty, you'd of had GPS!"

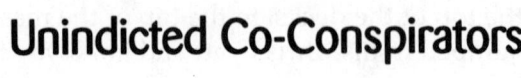

Unindicted Co-Conspirators

When the family travels by boat, it's great when everyone works together, as crew, to achieve a common goal. In most cases, reaching shore in one piece is a good common goal. If this shore happens to be a yet unexplored harbor, then that's great. These are good times afloat, when the crew works together.

But what about when one crew member is less than cooperative? Depending on who the crew member is, this can create anything from a minor inconvenience to a washed-out trip. I had similar problems myself this spring and I must tell you, this particular crew member went so far as to progress from "less than cooperative" to "full-blown mutinous" in a very short period of time. It ruined our first trip of the season. Chances are, you have a similar crew member aboard your own vessel. Let me tell you about my experience so that perhaps, you can nip-it-in-the-bud before it causes you grief.

The crew member that became contemptuous aboard Moonraker, was an engine. A standard V-8, gasoline-fed, marinized, mass-produced marvel. My relationship with this device started off this spring with a sleepy refusal to turnover. It progressed into a serious lack of communication and ended up in the hands of a labor relations expert: Bob, the mobile mechanic who brought some parts and lots of labor.

First, in all honesty, it is best to start out viewing the situation from the engine's perspective. Of all your crew members, your engine is the one in the worst physical condition. Face it, you keep him locked up in a poorly ventilated, isolation ward below decks. The poor guy is tube fed everything. You have his breathing gagged with a backfire flame arrestor. On top of all that, he's on electronic life support. He'll have anywhere from six to eight pacemakers implanted and suffer constant electric shock just to keep up a decent heart rate.

You are the one at the nurse's station supposedly monitoring his vital signs, but if the day is too pretty or the scenery too interesting...well it happens. There the poor engine is, locked away in a dark, stuffy room...cramped, on life support and generally ignored. Meanwhile, you sit in the bright sunshine and cool breezes with the horizon before you and the bikini-clad ones decorating the deck. This is the stuff revolutions are made of.

The changes may be subtle at first, a slight deterioration of their effort or an occasional hiccup. But be advised, the wildcat strike is in the works! Soon it will be slowdowns, intermittent work stoppages, entire days lost to the "blue flu" and then finally, an outright refusal to participate. That's mutiny!

And engines will use any excuse: "I don't like this fuel." "I'm hot." "I want a drink of water, now!" "My nose is all stuffy." "These tubes leak." "There's a monster in the bilge." You get the idea. They can be worse than the kids. But if you're a parent, you've learned how to tune them out too.

Try this, get two of them! They feel safer in numbers and I swear, as soon as you close the engine hatch, they start conspiring against you. First it's one, then the other in this tag team ritual meant to disturb and disrupt you. How much can you take? More correctly, how much can you give, because Bob can take a lot! I had some time to discuss counter tactics with Bob, as it is my practice to write slowly when the check calls for several zeros.

Just like your children, if you can anticipate their needs and complaints, you can take preventative measures to head-off a full blown engine temper tantrum. Example: When our children were small and we would take long car trips, my wife took responsibility for packing the passenger compartment of the car. She always made certain there were coloring books, games and even juice boxes for those thirsty with boredom.

Engines are the same way. On long trips, they like extra oil and coolant. Occasionally you have to change the oil while traveling (you wouldn't ask the baby to wait until you get home to be changed, now would you?) You should bring along extra clothes in case something should spoil what they have on (Hint: engines like to wear belts and hoses). And then there's food. In case your engine should develop colic, you should have extra filters along to strain baby's food. And of course, a full set of extra pacemakers is a must for the head nurse.

While this may sound silly, the premise works quite well. By anticipating your engine's needs, you can perform preventative maintenance on a predetermined schedule and solve the vast majority of your labor relations problems right there. And by expecting the unexpected, you can fight any wildcat strike that might occur with the proper tools and parts.

Confession time, my engine problems weren't this spring, but a year ago spring. At that time, it was my wife who took charge of the engine maintenance program aboard Moonraker. Not the doing of it, but the planning for it. Right after Bob left with that well-zeroed check, she actually read our engines' owners manual and took what she read to heart.

Stupid Boat Tricks

Just like planning a trip with the kids, she packed a bag with the spare engine parts recommended by the manual (imagine finding that information right there in of all places, the owner's manual!) She then started keeping a small log book of how many hours the engines were run as well as when scheduled service was due...and then done. It's been over a year now and I can tell you, Abbott and Costello (our port and starboard engines respectively) have never run better and this spring.., they turned over without a hitch! I can't tell what a joy it is to have these two fellows back as part of the crew. They are so much nicer then their evil twins, Khrushchev and Castro.

When the Captain Tossed His Cookies...

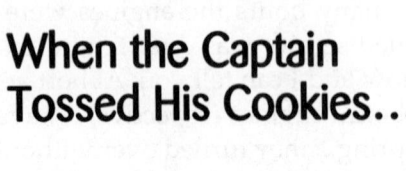

The ego is a powerful thing. And it can be a very powerful force when attached to an aggressive, over-achieving, sailboat racing captain/owner...especially when there's a bevy of bikini-clad babes on board. For our legal protection and my own personal safety, we will change the names here to protect the guilty: Since this stupid boat trick involves leadership, maturity and cookies, I shall refer to the star of this story as Captain Crunch, with all due apologies to the famed (and tasty!) breakfast food product, their representatives and of course, their legal staff.

It seems it was a hot, steamy day on Lake Huron, hazy, limited visibility...we've all been there. The good Captain was in the process of delivering his own racing boat from one port to the next in time for the next big competition. And what a craft she was! Sixty feet long with a space-age navigation station and dual helm positions with redundant meters, gauges and compasses...everywhere! There was room for a crew of twelve, but today, being just a delivery day, Captain Crunch was leisurely motoring his vessel across the open lake with only a handful of bikini-clad ones aboard for the ride. Life was good.

Yes, the Captain was in his element, casually sitting on the cockpit coaming enjoying what sunshine there was, almost as much as he was enjoying the attention of the ladies. They were well-offshore and far from the sight of land.

"Don't you need to do that navigation stuff?"

"No, not me. I've taken this route a hundred times. We'll just follow the compass."

"Don't you need to check our position with that GPS thing?"

"No, I know exactly where we are. Relax and enjoy lunch."

And so the day went. They puttered along through the haze as they ate lunch in the cockpit, just Captain Crunch and the ladies. To further impress them, for dessert, he produced a cookie tin stuffed full of delectable baked goods provided by his Mom. Every racing captain knows that women are turned-on by homemade baked goods and a guy who has a good relationship with his Mom! Besides, this was a fairly large cookie tin and was quite ornately decorated. Certainly the women would marvel over this too!

But it's a good thing the tin was big, and full, because the afternoon wore-on much longer than anticipated. Captain Crunch kept reassuring his crew that their intended harbor would pop out of the haze at any moment now...but in the mean time, just keep passing the cookies around. Finally, it was one of the beauties who asked the impertinent question:

"Why are we going in circles?"

"What? Impossible! I've been following this compass within three degrees all afternoon!"

But she pointed off the stern and sure enough, their wake showed a graceful arc of some considerable degree to port...

Captain Crunch looked at the compass. 90 degrees on the money! He quickly got up and stepped across the cockpit to the port-side helm position and looked at the redundant compass mounted there...123 degrees!? How could this be? He went back to the starboard side where he now had the undivided attention of every bikini on board and took another look at the compass...90...

Just then, one of the bevy picked up the cookie tin to

select yet another goodie for herself. And as she lifted it off the deck, the compass swung to 123 degrees. She passed the tin to a friend who also took another before setting it back down on the coaming. Now the compass read 40 degrees! Good old, "I don't need the navigation station," Captain Crunch had spent the afternoon chasing Mom's cookie tin across Lake Huron!

The bevy watched the good captain's face as he silently contemplated the true state of affairs. With all their meandering, he had no idea where they were. He hadn't done chart work in years. He raced, he helmed, he let the navigator worry about that stuff. The state of the art, fully-computerized navigation station? It was installed by the navigator.., whom the captain had dumped for the day so he would have the ladies to himself. There was a user's manual down there, somewhere…

In complete anger and frustration, Captain Crunch picked up the tin of cookies and flung the whole mess as far as he could out into Lake Huron. They all watched as some cookies floated and other cookies followed the tin to the bottom of the lake. There was silence among the crew.

Finally, one dejected bikini said, "Didn't your Mom want that tin back?"

Another said, "My Mom has one just like it…it's part of a set…"

With that, there was much nodding and lots of silence as the Captain struggled with the pencils and the dividers and somehow made sense of a GPS reading and eventually, they made port. But to this day, in the Pink Pony at the end of the Mac races, they still refer to this as the day Captain Crunch tossed his cookies. Even more embarrassing, guests who dine aboard this vessel have been known to feign asking for dessert just so they can add insult to injury:

"Do you have anything sweet on board, like maybe cake or cookies—Oh, that's right, your Mom won't let you!"

Nauticalese...

It all started when I decided to go to a local winter boat show. I love the boat show, I really do. And honestly, I like the winter ones more than the summer ones. There's just something about stepping in from the bitter cold and finding a hall filled with boats set up on pedestals like fiberglass gods. Seriously, it's great fun and the best kind of window shopping in the world. But something happened this year that made me view a few things differently.

Out in the parking lot, while trying to park my car amongst the mountains of freshly plowed snow, a group of boat show goers passed directly behind me on their way to the building's elevator and escalator system. One of them, realizing my car was still running and the backup lights were on, thumped my trunk with his hand and shouted out:

"Watch your stern!"

"Watch my stern?" I didn't know Chevys had sterns.

I know, I have heard references like this before. Hey, your talking to the guy here who invented "Winter Cruising" and coined the phrase, "Land Yacht." But there was just something about the way he said it.

I parked and followed this man and his small group to the show entrance. (Not because I planned to do him great bodily harm, but because we were on our way to the same boat show.) By the time we had shared space on the same elevator, several escalators and the grand hallway, I knew what it was that had bothered me.

The man was a "nautical name dropper." He had surrounded himself with a small group of fairly inexperienced boaters and was proceeding to intimidate, confuse and hopefully impress them with his vast boating expertise...conveyed through his sizable nautical vocabulary that he pounded, forced and contrived into nearly every sentence.

"Better stay abaft of that elevator door there or it'll catch you at the waterline!" he warned a woman in his group with a long, flowing coat as we all got on the elevator. He went on: "As soon as we get below, let's stow our coats and find a galley. My hold is mighty empty!"

He went on—actually he went on and on, but I'll spare you the nauseating details. The truth is, he spouted more nautical jargon than I have ever heard in my life and he managed to work it into the most unlikely sentences. He scrimshawed more ratlines onto the poop deck than had ever been pooped there before...but then, I just said that.

But he was impressing his friends. There were all nice folks from the suburbs come to "play boat." And every minute they hung around their captain here only made them more painfully aware that they had lots and lots to learn. I didn't have the heart (nor the opportunity) to tell them that the jargon he was using came out of one of those "ancient lore of the seas" books he probably bought at last year's show and spent the past twelve months memorizing. If you're a new boater, people like this can be intimidating.

It reminds me of a country club I once visited. It's a country club in the rolling suburban hills of a major Great Lakes city with several other facilities similar to it in the general vicinity. Similar to it in all but one aspect: This country club is on a lake. It's a small inland lake with a wee little island in the very middle that helps facilitate the rules of

Stupid Boat Tricks

navigation: everyone goes counterclockwise. On any given weekend, this large pond is a mixing bowl, churning with ski boats, jet skis, paddle boats and pontoons. And much like Alice Through The Looking Glass, there is not much place to go but around and around that big rock in the middle until you get where you're going. It's a lot like Indianapolis.

Yet, this country club, with its fine golf course, situated over an hour's drive from any body of water that's connected to any body of water that can remotely float a freighter...has chosen a nautical theme for its organization. And they take it very seriously! Their leader is a Commodore and their executive committee wears nautically-inspired uniforms that make my own Power Squadron uniform look like something from the Men's Warehouse, I guarantee it. Their uniforms are more of the Commodore Perry inspiration.. lots of brass and braid and so on.

Their clubhouse decor is also definitely nautical, but all saltwater nautical. There are sponges and nets and crabs on the walls. Paintings of Spanish Galleons in tropical hurricanes hang next to signs reminding you of the annual Neptune's Ball, just outside the doorway to Davey Jones' Locker (and bar). OK, so this can be fun. But what made me a brief visitor there was the pomp and circumstance that surrounded those who wear the uniforms. Again, I've never heard so much nautical jargon pooped on the deck by short-sheeted rigging monkeys who had never handled a poop before. And when they talked about the Commodore's fleet, they were referring to the handful of club-owned Sunfish Sailboards down on the private beach.

This is being nautical just for the sake of being nautical and if this is the closest you can get to the real thing, I guess there's no harm in it. What distresses me the most is that all too often, these Popeye-sound-alikes are given far more credibility then they actually deserve, simply because they can banter about some long forgotten words (ask your car mechanic about magneto windings).

The bottom line is this: If you're just getting into boating, welcome! You have just found a most enriching, rewarding and enjoyable pastime for the whole family. But you don't need to arm-wrestle with Popeye in order to be a respectable member of the flotilla. However, there are most definitely some things you should learn.

Put in a call to your local U.S. Power Squadron or Coast Guard Auxiliary. Both these fine groups teach a boating safety class that will allow you to skipper your craft with confidence while leaving all that scrimshawed salty stuff back in the Commodore's hat. Both these groups often have booths at your local boat show. Sign Up! Call your local boat store. Often they can point you in the right direction. I know as a fact that my own local BOAT/U.S. store helps out new boaters like this on a regular basis. Or you can just call 1-800-336-BOAT and get plugged-in to the national hot line. Then, call BOAT/U.S. Insurance, and you will find they will even give you a ten percent discount once you've completed the course.

Boating is a lot more fun when you know what you're doing. Knowing what you're doing is a matter of practical knowledge, not a bilge-full of enough salty expressions to belay a rickky-kneed rigging rat to the bow sprit...and that's no poop!

The Great Trailer Chase

There is no device ever invented by man that can intimidate, alienate, infuriate and totally embarrass quite the way a boat trailer can. Just when you think you've got it all figured out, it will find new ways to quietly let you know who's really in control. Let me give you a good example.

We shall call him Bill and he lives in rural, northeast Ohio along a nicely paved, country road. Bill bought a classic, 1952 Chris Craft runabout. After he did the mechanical restoration himself, he towed her on her brand new, tandem axle trailer, two miles up the road to Woodworker Wayne's house. Woodworker Wayne was an old school buddy of Bill's and he did hull and cosmetic restoration on boats like these.

One day in late August, Woodworker Wayne called Bill and reminded him yet again, that his Chris Craft was done, as good as new, and please, come and get it! You see, Bill had been busy and just hadn't gotten around to picking up this perfectly restored piece of nautical art. But in the face of an ultimatum, he promised to swing by that evening on his way home, about dusk.

But, as usual, Bill was running late and in a hurry. He only lived two miles down the road…so he decided to dispense with the time and effort required to attach the safety chains and just tightened the ball lock down tight. He jumped in the truck and eased her out onto the perfectly paved, recently resurfaced, two lane blacktop.

She was towing so well. Bill could see her back there in the mirrors, enhanced by the soft light of the tail lights. In fact, he was admiring her so much, he forgot about the only obstacle between him and home...the railroad tracks!

He hit them without slowing and it created an unusual sound and an unfamiliar shudder he could feel in the driver's seat. When he looked back in the mirror, he could still see the old Chris...though it was losing ground! The jolt of the tracks had unhitched the trailer from the Bronco and without the safety chains, this boat trailer had gone into business for itself.

It hadn't stopped. It was still rolling. The tandem axle trailer was precisely balanced for the boat. The wheels were straddling the crown of the perfectly paved road and occasionally, Bill could see sparks in the quickly advancing darkness as the skid on the trailer tongue lightly touched the surface of the road. His stomach sank. No matter how nicely this boat was riding the road now, he knew the only way this story could end was with a violent exit from the roadway, and a shower of splinters.

Bill suddenly remembered one more obstacle that stood between him and home...a hill. Like most hills, this one went both up and down, depending on which way you were coming. Unfortunately, in Bill's direction, it was all down hill from here. He looked back and noticed that the boat that was once falling behind, was now catching up...fast.

Now, if he let the boat catch up and rear end him, it would surely deflect off into the ditch and then find its way to the match factory. Besides, how could he explain to the insurance company that he had been rear ended by his own boat on a rural Ohio highway? If he just got out of its way, it would surely find a head-on collision with some poor, inno-

Stupid Boat Tricks

cent driver. No, his best bet was to let the trailer and the boat catch up, but stay out in front of it. That way, he could flash his lights at any on-coming traffic that might happen along until this story found an end.

Bill was amazed at how true the trailer was coasting. The occasional shower of sparks was the only indication that his classic boat was not indeed hitched to his truck. But now he had another concern. In order to keep just ahead of the trailer, Bill was forced to exceed the legally posted speed limit. Now, the speed limit was ridiculously low for this fine, straight piece of road, but it was a well known local speed trap for Deputy Dan, another old school mate of Bill's. Notice I didn't say school "chum."

It seems that back in grade school, Dan had earned the title of "Dan, Dan, the Tattletale Man" and his popularity had continued to decline from there. Today, he was a local Deputy Sheriff and frequently hid is squad car along this very stretch of road. How would Bill explain to Deputy Dan that he was speeding to escape his own trailer?

He would have to think fast, because behind him, behind the boat, from the darkness, appeared the tell-tale red and blue strobe lights that announced the arrival of Deputy Dan. Dutifully, Bill pulled over to the shoulder while the Chris Craft sped on down the road into the night.

Once he came to a stop, Deputy Dan was at the window in a flash.

"Bill! Bill! What about your boat trailer?" stammered the deputy.

"What trailer?" answered Bill in a calm, self-assured tone.

"The one you were towing! The one you were speeding with!"

"I wasn't towing a trailer. That was the Volkswagen behind me. And boy, was he in a hurry!"

"But that was your boat that's been up to Wayne's all

this time! I know that boat!"

"And I just sold it to some guy from Cleveland...who is towing it home with his VW..."

In confusion, Deputy Dan looked up the road into the darkness.

"Looks like he's long gone, now..." Bill added.

With a number of expressive phrases, Deputy Dan climbed back into his police car and returned back up the road to one of his preferred hiding places leaving Bill to secretly search for the wreckage of the lost boat.

But he didn't find any wreckage, just a pristine Chris Craft and trailer neatly parked on the gravely shoulder of the road a couple hundred yards from his own driveway. It seems, as the trailer slowed, it lost the momentum and balance that was keeping it on the crown of the road. As it drifted off to the right shoulder, it hit the soft gravel and slowed to a halt...unharmed.

Elated, Bill hooked up the trailer and quickly snuck the boat into his own barn before the lights on the police car could go off in Deputy Dan's head. It was there that Bill discovered the reason for this near tragedy: The day before, his sons had borrowed the Bronco and changed the trailer hitch ball to a smaller size...But didn't tell Dad and didn't put it back. Kids!

My Blue Poly

Well, here it is…the end of the season. By the time you read this, most of us will have put away our favorite toy for the Winter and the rest of you will be freezing your garbanzo beans off in the boat yard doing what we did last month.

No matter if your an "early outer" or frost bitten "hanger on," there is one thing we all have in common: Blue Poly. We all have to deal with it in some manner or other. Even if you leave your craft uncovered to the elements all Winter, you have at least dealt with it in the aspect of deciding to do without. Of those who won't do without, there are basically two kinds: The shrink wrappers and the tarpers.

The shrink wrappers are an interesting breed I have never been able to figure out. I think they're all descendants of Clarence Birdseye and I'll bet their galleys are lined with rows of canned goods. They like things well preserved. Every year they spend great sums of money to hermetically seal their craft in a vivid blue cocoon so that nothing but a few wisps of stray oxygen can find their way inside. Then they pay extra to have a door cut into the back so that something the size of a man in a snowmobile suit can enter with ease. I always found that odd. I bet their wives have refrigerators equipped with butter warmer compartments.

For those of you who don't know what a butter warmer is, well, it works like this: We build a box (a house) to keep the things warm because it gets cold outside. Then we build another box (a refrigerator) inside the first box to keep things cold. Then, inside that cold box, that's inside the warm box, we build another little box that will keep your butter warm and spreadable. I know about these things, my wife has one. Don't ask me, I just bought it for her.

I once had a conversation with a boater who liked shrink wrap. It went like this:

"So, you had your boat shrink wrapped..."

"Yup, all sealed up until spring. Nothin' gonna get in there."

"But there's a door...

"Well, that's so I can get in there."

"If it's all sealed up, why would you want to do that?"

"Well...If I start to run low on canned goods over the winter, I can come out here and get these off the boat!"

"And what do you do with all this stuff in the spring?"

"Well, you just cut it all up and throw it away!"

"Does your wife like the butter warmer in her refrigerator?"

"What?"

"So does mine..."

Personally, I buy the large blue poly tarps you can find at every boat store or home improvement center. Unfortunately, the home improvement centers never carry the size we with the bigger boats require, so that means it has to come from the boat store, and they know that!"

Tarping your boat can be a learning experience. If you wait until late in the season, you get to learn about frostbite and the inflexibility of plastic. If it's a windy day, you get to learn about aerodynamics and man's pursuit of flight. If you're an "early outer," you run the risk of doing your tarping during the heat of Indian Summer...and learning why they don't make pup tents from Blue Poly.

It can also be a chance to educate your children in the

ways of our culture and expand their understanding of the social order of things. Every time I tarp my boat, I think back to a time just a few years ago when my then young daughter asked me:

"Daddy, is our boat dead?"

Frustrated by rather expensive late-season engine repair that wouldn't be completed until spring, I sarcastically answered:

"Yes, Sweety. It's dead...but we'll cover it up and it will be all better next spring."

It wasn't until later that winter that I realized how unfortunate that remark was. I was called into my daughter's room by my wife to help her search for the source of a foul odor that had been present for several days. There, under the bed, we found a very neat row of perhaps a half dozen dead gold fish, each hiding under a small square of blue construction paper. This baffled us. So we asked the little princess what they were doing there, to which she replied with her finger to her lips: "Shhhhh...they're waiting for spring!"

Perhaps the shrink wrappers have something there after all. Or maybe it's just my own frustration at the end of another boating season. Maybe we should all move to Florida and never buy blue poly again. But no...then we'd have to put coolers on our butter warmers to keep our butter from melting in the refrigerator. Such is life...

So What's for Dinner?

Recently, I had dinner with Ken Miller and Bruce Jenvey. As it often does, the memory of our good friend Jon Kaplan came up and changed the course of meal time conversation. What I am about to share with you is a truly classic stupid boat trick, one of Jon's all-time favorite stories and one we have laughed about a lot over the years. I only wish you readers could hear Jon tell it, but I will do my best to do this story justice.

Jon once worked as the "Quality Control Director" (read: chief repair guy for warranty work) at a major boat dealership. In essence, it was his job to solve the problems of new boaters with brand new boats. We all know that automobiles need a few corrections and adjustments when they leave the dealership, but you'd be surprised how many people expect their boat to be perfect. Making them perfect was what Jon did best.

Once, the salesman handed him the keys to a rather large and expensive luxury sailboat that had only been in service a month and had come back for warranty work. There were two complaints: The bilge pump seemed to run far too often...check for hull and fitting leaks, and, the refrigeration unit didn't seem to be working right. Food stored there took on an unsavory flavor.

Jon went to work. First things first, he checked the bilge.

Stupid Boat Tricks

There was a good amount of dark, brackish, bilge water down there, not enough to make the pump run yet, but too much to see where any trickles might be leading from. Since there was no impending sinking, he moved on to the refrigerator.

Now remember, this was a cruising sailboat. Like most craft of its kind, it had a combination refrigerator/ice box, meaning you could run the refrigeration unit and/or, throw in a block of ice or a bag of cubes. Access into the unit was through the counter top (too keep the cold air from spilling out when opened) with a drain in the bottom that was directed to the bilge.

Jon opened the top and peered down into the vast, empty space. Even now, there was a distinctive odor of past meals gone bad. He pondered. He flipped the breaker and activated the refrigeration unit. It kicked in and within a couple of minutes, there was a noticeable change in the cooler's temperature. He looked into the cooler some more. He pondered, and sniffed again.

Just then, the automatic bilge pump triggered and Jon could hear the faithful little pump whirring away beneath his feet. But to his amazement, right before his eyes, the entire bottom half of the cooler filled with the dirty, brackish water from the bilge! That was the odor! When the pump ceased, the water stood there for sometime, slowly draining back from where it came, only to repeat the process again. He timed it.

It was apparent to Jon what had happened. There are usually three hoses leading into the bilge: one from the shower sump, one from the cooler drain and the one you hook the output of the bilge pump to so that everything goes out over the side. To save money, boat builders order hose in bulk and use the same color and style hose for all these jobs.

Someone at the factory had mistakenly hooked the output of the bilge pump to the cooler drain...Rather than expelling the bilge water, this boat was recycling it, and letting it "steep and mature" with every running of the pump. Not only that, but these particular new boat owners were marinating the entire contents of their cooler in this concentrated bilge water several times a day. Well, they say food cooked aboard does taste different from that cooked at home.

Jon Kaplan used to love to tell this story just before the burgers came off the grill and would end it with a beaming: "So, what's for dinner?" Sadly, the burgers just haven't been the same since he's been gone...

Four-Legged Cruisers

How many of you out there travel with pets? Or should I ask, how many of you out there have pets? And I'll bet there's a difference in the hand count we get on those two questions.

Personally, we have a four-legged crew member of the dog variety. A small, hairy creature that answers to the name of Gilligan. Don't blame me, blame my then six and eight year old children's addiction to cable television. Actually, they wanted to take the whole litter and re-unite the entire crew of the Minnow. I got them to settle for just Gilligan. Obviously, we were boaters before we were pet owners, but there's no reason it couldn't have been the other way around.

I grew up with dogs on the water. When I was a kid, we had a family cottage on a big inland lake not so far from the house that we couldn't drive out there for an afternoon or an evening and of course, every weekend. We also had a standard dachshund named Reinhart that loved the lake I think even more than we did. He was smart enough that if he heard the word "lake," he was all excited and all ready to go...and when we resorted to spelling "L-A-K-E" in his presence, he responded by learning that too.

He was a character. He would love to lay in the sun next to the dock for hours on end. He loved rides in the ski boat with ears flying and his tongue hanging down to China.

And the pontoon boat...On cool evenings we would take a lazy ride around the shore line while he curled up in a blanket with nothing but his over-sized schnoz extended like a snorkel, catching every scent, every breeze, at every change of direction.

Reinhart loved the lake, as does Gilligan and every other dog who has ever been to the shore. And people like having their pets around! I met a couple one weekend at Boblo that never went anywhere without their two cats on board their 25 foot Catalina sailboat. I know another couple that lives aboard a Grand Banks Trawler for six months out of every year with "Chip," a rather hair-brained "perpetual puppy" of some small equestrian breed. Jon and Kay often go sailing with "Winston," the feline version of Jabba The Hut. Ken Miller has a small German Shepherd named "Nugget" (He also had a cat named "Frog" but that's another story), and even the publisher of this magazine does a very interesting Long John Silver impression with a small wiener dog perched on his shoulder.

I bring these people to your attention in contrast to those you always see leaving the marina early, those who never spend the night and those who very rarely travel on their boats. And when you ask them why, it's because they have to get home for the pet...The pet (usually a dog) got left at home and by now needs attention. It seems cats take care of themselves.

This trend intrigued me, so I started my own unscientific survey. It seems that the vast majority of people who leave their pets at home, had the pet before they had the boat. Many are convinced the pet won't adapt to the marine environment. Some actually tried it once...and decided the pet would be happier at home. And then there's a small segment that is afraid what the pet will do to the interior of the prize possession. I say it all sounds like Bull.

Your pet is a member of the family. He can adapt to boating just as your children did. You wouldn't leave your small daughter at home just because she got scared or a little nauseated the first time out, would you? Then why leave the four legged family member? If he's truly happy just to be with you, he will be happy with you wherever you go. You just have to take a few things into consideration:

When introducing an older pet to your newer passion of boating, move slowly. Take him out there and let him discover the lake and all its smells at his pace. Maybe the first weekend you don't leave the dock.

If your pet is nervous in the cockpit or up on the flybridge, send him below for a while. He'll probably curl up and nap. He may do this every time you leave the dock.

If your pet becomes nauseated below, bring him up into the fresh breezes and keep him comforted with a pat on the head and a reassuring voice. He will eventually adapt.

Reduce your guilt stress factor by cleaning up after your pet. A plastic bag inverted over your hand is quick, easy and clean. My eleven year old actually finds it fun...

Make time at the lake to do the thing your pet likes best, just as you would include the things your child or spouse like to do. Mine loves an evening walk all the way down the canal to the water tower followed by a nice romp on the lawn (my dog, not my spouse, but she likes to come along).

And for those of you who are afraid what a pet would do to the inside of your boat, I have these closing comments for you: I'll bet your pet doesn't have a good time at home either. Your boat should be an extension of your family room, not your parlor. It should be a facet of your life style, not an expression of your self image. If you're afraid to mess up your boat, you're not doing it right.

Walking in a Winter Wonderland...

By the time you read this, it will be November. Our late spring, short summer and early fall will have produced one of the most vivid color seasons in years and we will be standing on the edge of another Great Lakes winter. Rejoice! I know the boat may be up on blocks and shrink-wrapped, but you're not!

It was nearly three years ago that I introduced the idea of "Winter Cruising." I'm glad to say that not only is the magazine still here, but this idea of Winter Cruising has really caught on too. For those of you new to the concept let me give you the rules:

Winter Cruising involves taking the same luggage you hauled around last summer, packing many of the same clothes (ix-nay on the shorts, take the jeans instead) and throwing it all into the trunk of the Land Yacht—that ship of the highways you keep next to the house.

For those of you unfamiliar with Land Yachts, they are amazing devices. If you're a sailor, you'll be amazed at how fast they are. Why, some of them do fifty, even sixty miles an hour! And if you're a powerboater, you'll be astonished at your fuel economy. You might even save enough money on gas to pay for a bed & breakfast for the whole weekend.

But where to go? Well, you know all those small harbor towns you explored last summer? You'd be surprised just how many of those towns are right there in the same place all winter long. And lots of 'em are open too! Don't expect to play mini-golf or buy an ice cream cone, but believe it or not, there are other things in life.

Don't get me wrong. I'm not big on winter sports. I have often questioned the sanity of anyone who straps boards to their feet and slides down a hill. Snowmobiles are just another annoying cousin of the jet ski. And snowshoes? Putting tennis rackets on my feet is not my idea of a fashion statement. Wind-chill factor…frostbite…black ice…snowdrifts. Makes you want to stay near the roaring fire in your favorite turtleneck with a mug of hot chocolate at hand, doesn't it? And what if that roaring fire had a picturesque view with an easy stroll to a couple of nice shops and a restaurant? Now you're talking Winter Cruising! But where can you find such a place?

Right in the pages of your old *Great Lakes Cruiser* magazines! Pick a town, any town, and for the most part, you'll find that bed & breakfast or resort hotel listed under places to stay. You'll probably enjoy a nice off-season rate too. And if you read further, you'll also discover things to do specific to the season…or we at least tell you where to find that information. Dare me to name just a handful of prime Winter Cruising destinations?

Just hopping around the lakes off the top of my head, how about Port Washington, Wisconsin? A beautiful village, great shopping and some nice downtown accommodations. Too far for many of us by boat, but at seventy-land-yacht-miles-per-hour…it's a nice weekend away. If you go in early December, you'll see the Christmas parade with a European-style St. Nicholas and his helpful side-kick, Black Peter. They pass out chocolate coins to the children (just the good ones, according to Black Peter's book). It's quite a sight with that big church up on the hill and the town all decorated…

If that's too far, try Milwaukee with its Flemish architecture and first-class micro-breweries. And don't forget to tour the big breweries too! If you want something on a smaller scale, try Racine. There's a bed & breakfast there with the roaring fire and the view of Lake Michigan you've been looking for.

Maybe you want a secluded weekend away. Up in Keweenaw territory, you can find both the Sand Hills and Big Bay Lighthouses. Both are bed & breakfasts now and since they were both active lightstations at one time, they just happen to have an unforgettable view of Lake Superior. Pour the hot chocolate and watch a winter storm rage on the open waters.., all from the snug safety of your lighthouse.

But wait, there's more! Visit the Grand Traverse Bay area of northern Michigan and pick the weekend experience you want most; Stay in busy downtown Traverse city, or try out one of the smaller, outlying towns. Stay where you want but visit them all. They're all only a short Land Yacht cruise away!

Chatham, Ontario, is just off Lake St. Clair, and there you'll find the Wheels Inn. This is a tremendous, entirely indoor resort. And if you're brave enough, there's lots of quaint shopping just outside the doors.

Here's a few more favorites: Go spend a victorian weekend in Canada at Niagara-on-the-Lake. The Queen's Parkway is a beautiful drive and the falls are just minutes away. Have you ever seen Niagara Falls in the winter? There are lots of places to stay around here, but if you want to sample one of the more unique experiences in the area, try the historic Olde Angel Inn.

Even farther east, you can always drive up to Port Hope for the weekend. If you like all things victorian, this is the place for you! Shops, jewelry stores and antiques are all around you.

But don't forget about the Trent-Severn! Both Bobcaygeon and Fenelon Falls are prime examples of quiet

Stupid Boat Tricks

Canadian Villages enjoying a slower pace of life until the summer season comes again. And if you want bigger city entertainment, there's always Peterborough or even Orillia. Don't forget, Orillia now has that big beautiful casino for those who like their action with an element of risk.

And there are lots and lots of other places around every corner of the lakes. The point here is that the Great Lakes region enjoys four distinct seasons, each with it's own beauty. If you're traveling only during one of them, you're missing a lot! So I encourage you to find your own favorite roaring fire with a view of the open lake and make that Land Yacht voyage this winter. And if you haven't taken the hint already, you just might find another member of your crew who'd like to go along too...

Lose Your Breakfast at Tiffany's

Here's an interesting observation: During an impromptu rendezvous on the lakes last summer (about half of our staff wound up in the same harbor on the same night) I noticed a number of our party wearing those elastic wrist bands with the plastic bump that are supposed to prevent motion sickness.

You know the ones I'm talking about. They're sold under a couple of different brand names but they are the same, fabric-covered elastic bands in your choice of blue or gray. I guess the color choices allow you to proudly display your Civil War loyalties because neither color seems to match my flesh tone very well. Maybe if I were a zombie or an arctic explorer…neither of which would seem to have a problem with motion sickness. But back to my observation.

Like I said, several members of our party were wearing them. There was Chris Jenvey, Bob Swanson and well…me. I admit, I occasionally wear them. Perhaps that's why I observe them so quickly on other people. And if they're not wearing them, you can always see that telltale red indent on their wrists.

The truth is, I have always been prone to motion sickness and I've tried all the remedies. The pills make me sleepy, the patches can't seem to get through my thick skin, but the wrist bands work! My full-time job often puts me on an airplane so I always fly with the bands. Long car trips where

Stupid Boat Tricks

I'm the passenger can be a problem, so I take them along. And I always wear them on the boat on days I'm expecting rough seas. But I am terribly self-conscious about wearing them and even hours later in the restaurant, find myself hiding the little red marks on my wrists left by the plastic, acu-pressure ball.

It finally occurred to me, that night when we were all in the restaurant, that with just a little creativity, these "red badges of green courage" could be made into things of beauty and style. The last time I was in New York, I contacted the Tiffany people. They were a little shocked at first, but then listened to my ideas with increasing interest.

Think of it. You could replace your standard blue or gray band with the plastic bump with, let's say, a golden watchband with a Cartier timepiece under which was concealed the stomach-calming bump. For the ladies, golden bracelets with antique cameos to serve as the acu-pressure point. They could even be diamond encrusted. Sure! You've heard of anniversary rings...one diamond for each year of marriage. How about encrusting your spouse's watchband or bracelet with one diamond for every time they had lost their breakfast while crossing Lake Erie?

And here's a cure for those embarrassing red indents left on your wrists: Simply carve the logo of the jewelry's designer into the bottom of the pressure ball, in reverse. That way, when you take them off, you will have designer indents! Imagine little red circles on your wrists that say Tiffany, Dior or Calvin Klein! It could be most impressive and for once and for all, remove the stigma of those little elastic wrist bands...

Night of the Beagle

Though dog may be man's best friend, not all dogs were cut out for the cruising lifestyle. Let me tell you, very painfully, of one such example. In my marina, this is an incident that has come to be known as "The Night of the Beagle" and is only mentioned in hushed tones.

It was a beautiful, mid-summer weekend in our marina. About noon, on Saturday, up drove Dave and the family. Dave keeps his boat just a couple slips down from me and they always attend all our marina get-togethers. We know them well. However, this weekend, they were one plus...In tow, they had a dog.

Now, I like dogs. We travel with a dog. Gilligan, the aging shitzu, is a regular member of our crew and has been all his life. We brought him on board when he was a pup and he took to this boating thing just fine. I can say the same for several other of our staffers too. Dogs are nice to have on board!

But this dog was different. He was mostly beagle...and a pup of just under a year old. His name was Arlo, after the original hippie-hobo, Arlo Guthrie...a creation of the American mixing pot. The most important thing to emphasize here is that Arlo was not Dave's dog. Dave and his family were only dog-sitting Arlo for the weekend while his regular victims were out of town. Arlo, was a loaner dog.

Stupid Boat Tricks

Things had seemed to start well. Arlo was glad to see everyone and anyone who would scratch his ears. And he was ready to play a creative version of fetch with the equally tireless youngsters. My first clue that there might be a problem was in the dog's failure to grasp the basic concept of fetch. Half the time, the kid would throw the stick, the dog would chase up to it and bark at it, run back to the kid and bark at the kid until the kid went and got the stick. Then they'd throw it again. The dog would play the game in the expected manner just often enough to keep the kids trying. You could call it creative, cute, stupid, manipulative, even diabolical...but it was an indication of things to come.

The happy family got on board their precious boat with their loaner dog and began to set out the cushions and the toys. There was a touch of excitement in the air as Dave had been wanting a dog and this would be a trial weekend, judging all canines in general against this one. If they ever got a dog or not depended on how this weekend went.

Within minutes, there was a shriek from the cabin. "What the—!" It seems the puppy was nervous and without realizing it, had confused his chewy toy with one of the First Mate's salon cushions. A hole had been chewed! Arlo was sent to the cockpit while the smoke cleared. It was only a pillow, not a custom cushion. It was replaceable.

"The poor puppy has never been on a boat before. He misses his people and he's nervous."

All the usual excuses were made and a wave of forgiveness was creeping through the cabin. That is, until they all came out to the cockpit to comfort the poor, confused, nervous puppy...only to realize that in the ten minutes he was unattended, he had chewed a corner off the nearest cockpit cushion.., custom made in coordinating colors.

The shrieking and yelling resumed and the dog, completely oblivious to the unhappiness he had caused, was banished to the shore. He was chained (I now realize why this dog had no leash. He had come to them with a chain.), I said he was chained to the picnic table in the shade at the bow of the boat. In exasperation, Dave tried to salvage the day by suggesting repairs to the spoiled cushion and consoling his wife about the damage to the boat. This took some time, but not that much time.

This conversation ended with the boat abruptly bumping a dock piling. "That's odd," thought Dave. He always had the boat tied just so, to give a comfortable ride at the dock. He looked over the side of the boat and examined his lines from the stern to the bow— There, at the bow, a dockline hung limply in the water. And the other end? Part of it was still tied to the sea wall, and the other part was in Arlo's mouth. In only a few minutes, this dog had chewed through a 3/8-inch nylon dockline

"Arlo!" Dave shouted and in response, the dog dropped the dockline and jumped up on all fours with his tail wagging. He was ready to play any game Dave was ready to start.

Upon examination and replacement of the dockline, Dave discovered a whole foot of dockline was missing...and so was a section of his slipmate's water hose.

"Good thing he didn't chew the shore power cord, Dad!" piped up one of the kids. Dave was starting to wonder.

Arlo spent the rest of the day on a shorter chain near the picnic table with his food and water dishes near at hand. He gladly accepted pets and ear scratches from anyone passing by, completely oblivious to the destruction he had caused. He was just having a great time!

That night, he found himself across the marina driveway with the boat trailers. He was securely fastened to a carefully-measured chain and anchored to the largest trailer there. In the early evening, he barked and howled and kept most of us awake. But we didn't complain, knowing that anyone who took pity on him might literally be eaten out of house

Stupid Boat Tricks

and home.

In the morning, we were all met with the most amazing sight. Here was that happy-to-see-you, beagle mutt, still chained to the trailer...but the trailer was no longer where it had been left. While we had slept, this amazing dog had somehow managed to tow that trailer the two feet necessary to expand his reach of chewable objects. What had he chewed in the night? Arlo had chewed every electrical connector off every trailer in that part of the lot. Five of them to be exact and what's more, two of the smaller, plastic connectors were never found. A child's life jacket, hung over a trailer tongue to dry, had been partially devoured. Oddly, when the pieces were gathered together, there was obviously a significant amount of missing foam and filler. The topper: The dog had eaten part of Dave's minivan! The extra reach he had gained by pulling the trailer out of line, had allowed him to reach the plastic trim along the left rear wheel-well of the van. Black must have been Arlo's favorite color, as a good portion of the trim was gone, and there were only scraps of it on the ground.

In disgust and surrender, Dave packed up the family that morning with intentions of returning home early. As he loaded the last of the bags into the remains of his van, one of the more senior residents of our little marina came by and watched.

"Goin' home, are ye, Dave?" he asked.

"Yup" was the solemn reply.

"Takin' that dog with ya?"

"Yup" was the answer again.

"Good..." said the old man. "I don't know exactly what went into that dog, but I sure don't want to be around when it comes out!"

To this day, we speak of Arlo's only-ever visit to the marina in hushed tones and refer to it as "The Night of the Beagle." Dave never got a dog and whenever you ask him what's on the grill tonight, the answer we've come to expect, is beagle-burgers....

Burnt Offerings

I don't consider myself a chauvinist. I have always believed in a fair and equitable division of duties at home. True, I do the yard work, repair the house and maintain the cars, but these traditionally male roles falling upon my shoulders were my wife's decisions. And if a woman decided it, how can it be chauvinistic, right?

But I also help out inside the house too. I do laundry, sometimes. I can vacuum and I know the business end of a dust rag. Again, a decision made by my wife. But one thing I don't do is cook. More correctly, I am not allowed to cook. This is to everyone's relief and well being, even my own.

I'm sorry, but there just seems to be no aptitude within me for the culinary sciences. Most everything I attempt winds up either a gooey mess or a burnt offering for the gods.

And it's not that I don't want to either. From time to time, I used to sneak into the kitchen and take a shot in the dark at whipping up something truly special for my family. My great hope was that just once, I'd hit the magic combination of ingredients, temperature and time resulting in "The Big One." The "One" that would wipe away all my past failures and stand as my own personal mark of excellence.

After my last "Big One," my wife called the EPA. Now,

my kitchen privileges are limited to making coffee, pouring milk and doing dishes. You can't fight the federal government and now I can't cook for them either.

So tell me, why is it, when you take a guy like me, put me in a marina and light a BBQ grill, why does my own wife hand me several dollars worth of meat and the weapons to wreak vengeance? What mystical transmutation is supposed to take place when the kitchen is moved outdoors that suddenly qualifies me to prepare things for human consumption? Remember, I'm a government certified hazard to the environment!

Sadly, I must inform you that there is no mystical transmutation. Try as I might, the only thing ever to come out of my BBQ was a disaster. And I have heard all the jokes!

"Hey, Tonto! What do those smoke signals say?"

"Will this be a three alarm or a four alarm cookout?"

"Only you, can prevent this Barbecue!"

"My, the Gods will be pleased!"

I've tried everything. I've cooked strictly by stopwatch, by smell, with my watchful wife just a few paces away. Still we suffer the indignities of eating carbonized meat in public. The black powdered smudges around our mouths tell it all.

"Aren't those ribs a little over done there, J.K.?" asks a nosy passerby.

"It's pork. You can't be too careful with pork..."

The final indignation came just this past Memorial Day weekend when an over abundant amount of grease from some hamburgers I was desecrating decided to ignite. Somehow, the flaming grease found its way out through the vent holes in the bottom of my table-top gas grill and involved the plastic table cloth covering my picnic table in the sacrifice. When plastic burns, things get nasty. The people around you get nasty too. In a matter of seconds, I went from innocently incinerating my burgers to being the center of attention and the victim of a series of rapid events that ended with several water soaked people, one empty fire extinguisher and a request from the marina manager that my wife run the barbecue from now on.

She and I had a long discussion that night. After we ruled out moving to another marina where nobody knew us, we got down to the reason why this whole mess happened in the first place. Funny thing, it seems I had been suffering public ridicule of my cooking expertise for one reason and one reason only: Conformity. All the other husbands in the marina did the BBQ thing, and in an effort to be one of the crowd, she felt I should too.

It seemed so silly. All our lives together, we had prided ourselves on being the non-conformist couple, from our radical college days to our current non-traditional stance in the suburban neighborhood. But here we were, engaging in activities and roles not suited to us, in an effort to be someone we weren't...amazing. And the strangest part of all is that we were letting this get in the way of our own enjoyment.

We learned from our lesson. She now runs the grill while I do just about anything else around the dock that doesn't involve preparing food. We're happier, we're eating better and our friends in the marina sleep peacefully on weekend nights. But it makes me wonder about how many other people out there might be trapped in similar role games. Let me offer these words of advice:

With only a few small exceptions, there really is no "wrong" or "right" way to do this boating thing. I mean, it is considered bad form to run aground, sink or succumb to fire. But other than that, there aren't a whole lot of rules! You come out to your boat to escape the rigors and rules of society, why impose new ones on yourself whenever you set foot in the marina? I guess the whole bottom line here is be yourself. Don't try to "fit in" and don't play "keep up with the Popeyes."

There will always be someone who can do some aspect of this whole thing better than you. That's to be expected. The fact that he has to prove it to everyone proves a whole lot more about him than just his expertise. Let it ride. Pull up a nice Adirondack chair and sacrifice something to the gods with my compliments.

They'll Always Come Out to Get You…

You'll pardon me if I deviate from my usual light-hearted approach this month, but Jenvey got a letter. It was a short but scathing little missive that condemned the actions of that despicable band of storm troopers known as the United States Coast Guard. Well, at least according to the writer. Instead of letting this one pass through the mailboat section, I thought I'd take it, and tell you a story.

A long time ago, all around the Great Lakes, there was a whole lot of nothing. Towns and villages were few and far between and more often than not, there were no roads connecting them to the outside world. What they had, were the lake boats. Those brave sailors of the lakes brought the news, the people and the products that were the life blood of the community.

But the lakes were known to turn angry and many a good ship and crew were lost, sometimes without a trace. In response to these tragedies, there was formed the United States Life Saving Service. These were handfuls of brave young men stationed at remote facilities all around the shores of these great inland seas. They gave up many of life's creature comforts to be a part of this service, and I can tell you they certainly didn't do it for the money.

Their job was quite simple, really. They would answer the call of distress from anyone, anytime, in any weather, without regard for personal safety. They would take to the lake in small boats on the darkest of nights, in the coldest of weather in an effort to save just one life. "They did what?" you ask again.

I said, they would always come out to get you. It could be a pitch black night on an unlit shore. There could be a November gale blowing hard enough to cripple and condemn a three-hundred-foot package freighter. And these young men would set out from the shore, into the freezing darkness, in a small boat with nothing but oars and life jackets. Then they'd proceed to pluck half dead sailors from the water. They'd go below the decks of burning steamers and drag out those who had given themselves up for lost. They were the Life Saving Service, and they were always prepared, and they would always come out to get you. And the sailors knew it too. So many shipwreck stories include the doomed ship frantically sounding her steam whistle while running parallel to the shore. This was an attempt to get the attention of anyone who would then call out the Life Savers...because they knew, they'd always come out to get you.

There are far more tales of heroism and resourceful action associated with this service than we could begin to tell you about. After all, venturing out into a storm ravaged lake is risky business and sometimes, they all didn't come back. But those that did brought with them the souls they had saved and the stories of the souls that were lost.

In 1915, the U.S. Life Saving Service became the United States Coast Guard and while names may change and responsibilities become larger, some things remain the same.

Several years ago, I was with Jenvey and his oldest son as we took his new boat on a shake-down, overnight for "just the guys." Stiff winds became a full gale and we were pounding our way into the thick of it towards the shelter of the shore when we encountered a small, overturned boat with two men who were desperately trying to flip their craft back over. For whatever reasons, they declined our offer to climb aboard when we passed by them. We knew we couldn't turn around, not without endangering our own craft and crew. And we knew they would never get that small boat upright, let alone back to shore.

We called the Coast Guard on the VHF and within minutes, a small boat came crashing across the waves to pull two, half frozen, half drowned weekend skippers from the lake. They'll always come out to get you.

Just two or three years ago, as a storm raged on Lake Erie, some mental defective called in a prank mayday on his VHF from the comfort and the safety of his own marina. Of course, he claimed to be lost and sinking out on the big lake. Again, the brave young men piled into the little boat and went out into the worst of it because that's what they do. They'll always come out to get you. This time, one of them didn't come back. And despite the arrest and conviction of the prankster, and given every reason on earth to stay in the bunk when the alarm goes off the next time, they remain "always prepared" because it's their job to come out and get you.

So, Mr. Letter Writer, I will allow you to remain nameless. But the next time you feel like complaining because some exhausted "Coastie" knocked over your cooler or put a scuff in your deck in an effort to save your backside, please remember that he was there. Remember that, like his predecessors, he was standing by the ready when you called for help. And always remember, that he will always come out to get you...

Commander Ma'am

A stupid boat trick can find any victim.., any victim. No person is above an act of questionable judgment. It can happen to anybody, and in this case, I have been asked to keep the anybody nameless...to the best of my ability. We shall call her Commander Ma'am.

Let me tell you about Commander Ma'am. She is a responsible and well-trained boater. She grew up on the water. She is the past leader of her local boating organization. She teaches boating safety. She is the veteran of many a long-distance sailboat race and even more boating deliveries from across the Great Lakes to all sections of the Caribbean. She has weathered the worst the lakes could throw at her and she keeps coming back for more.

When a certain, well-known writer needed an extra skilled hand to take his own boat from winter storage, around the lakeshore to its summer berth, Commander Ma'am gladly volunteered to help.

This was a several-day trip and the well-known writer was immediately impressed with her skills. She had never seen this boat before but by the end of the second day, she had become most comfortable with the boat's helm, she had mastered most of the multi-function electronics and had even started a list of maintenance items that needed attention...what a woman!

Stupid Boat Tricks

But near the end of the third day, the weather had grown most foul. The temperature was in the low 40s, thirty-knot breezes and five-foot waves sent freezing spray over the bow and a dangerous level of fatigue was setting in on the well-known writer at the helm.

Commander Ma'am took action as only she knew how. She took the helm. Their intended destination was still hours away, but enough was enough. She headed the boat ashore for an unscheduled stop and good night's rest at the harbor of refuge right then off their beam. Through the churning seas, she did a masterful job at bringing this unfamiliar, multi-ton craft around the sandbar and shot the gap through the breakwaters...the only protection there was from the open, angry lake.

It was agreed, she would dock the boat. The well-known writer was too exhausted—she was in the best condition to bring them safely in. The information she needed was quickly transferred: 12,000 pound vessel, full-length keel, single screw, right-hand prop will walk the stern to the left in low reverse, warm-idle: 875 RPM...you get the idea.

It was at this time, with one hand on the wheel, one hand on the hand-held VHF (and I think there was something about a dockline in her teeth), that Commander Ma'am radioed their approach and dockage request to the harbormaster's office. But what she hadn't planned on was how well-known the well-known writer was. By the time they approached their assigned dockage, four people who had recognized the boat's name were already on the dock to greet them with more on the way. Out in front of them all, was the harbormaster himself!

Even with this pressure, Commander Ma'am did a masterful docking job. The exhausted writer took a dockline forward and waited as she swung the boat into the slip. With an unfamiliar vessel under her feet and thirty knots of breeze on her beam, she brought the boat into the slip without brushing a piling! The writer felt the craft hesitate as she shifted to reverse, and then it walked to port as it came to dead stop, barely tapping the piling.

The writer had made such a wonderful entrance to this harbor that he was beaming as he handed the now, overly-long dockline directly to the harbormaster himself. The other end had already been secured to the bow cleat. The harbormaster was beaming too. He exuberantly greeted the well-known writer and immediately started making dinner invitations, offers for use of motor vehicles and office equipment for his guest.

"We are very pleased to be here," said the writer. "But we seem to be leaving..."

And he was right! Just as perfectly as the boat had docked, it was now inching away in reverse and gaining speed. The overly-long dockline was now a tangled mess in the harbormaster's arms. It grew taut.

The writer looked back at the helm, some thirty feet away, to see why they were leaving. But there was no one at the helm. Commander Ma'am was away from the wheel handing docklines to the assistant harbormaster...and had left the gear shift in reverse! As soon as the error was realized, she scrambled for the helm but some things just happen too fast.

The writer looked back at the harbormaster who had run out of all slack, and was now literally wrapped-up in the tangled mess. BOINK! The harbormaster was rudely introduced to piling number one. He some how managed to get the line over the top of the pole and back on the dock side. Let's see...12,000-pound boat, 23 horsepower engine, 30-knot breeze against a 165-pound harbormaster...not gonna happen. BOINK! The harbormaster met piling number two but was unable to get the dockline over the top of this one and decided to refresh himself in the harbor instead.

By now, Commander Ma'am had the vessel once again

under control. Without tension on the line, the harbormaster was freed and the growing crowd hefted his dripping form back onto the dock. Commander Ma'am turned a lovely shade of red. To make light of an embarrassing situation, the well-known writer made a comment about the water "looking real cold."

Without hesitation, Commander Ma'am pressed the correct button on the multi-function cockpit meter and announced to all present, "Yes, its forty-four degrees down there."

Like the shivering harbormaster needed to hear that...

The Survivalist

This is the winter of our discontent. Actually any winter meets with my discontent. At least it feels that way in January when we have the bulk of it staring us right in the snow shovel. January...The only thing worse than just January is early January because that means you have to count it when you count how many months to launch date. Months to launch date...doesn't that sound terrible? It seems like it will be forever before we start talking about launch day in terms of weeks, and then in days.

I tried to circumvent that feeling last winter by refusing to recognize the months to launch day status and went straight on to weeks instead. A process of mind over matter it seemed to me. But no one wanted to talk to a guy who babbled incoherently about "14 weeks to launch." Especially one obviously prepared to do so for the next 14 weeks. Not even my day planner wanted to go up that far.

It is out of frustrations such as these that true creative genius is born. This year, I have developed a plan. Something I call The Survivalist's Plan to Winter. Yes, I dare invoke the name of those lovable crazies predominantly from northern California who dug trenches, buried food and stockpiled weapons against the very visible threat of the Armageddon du Jour. They were prepared for just about any calamity except Sal Manila and federal gun laws. Yet in

Stupid Boat Tricks

their memory, I put forth the following suggestions to survive the season of no surf:

1. Stockpile all your non-permanently attached boating equipment in your basement for the winter. This offers several advantages. Here, it is safe from boat thieves (house-type thieves tend to look at this stuff, not know what it is and proceed on to your TV, Stereo, VCR and jewelry. Smart, huh?). You can also keep an inventory close at hand if questions should arise as to what you do and don't have. This is also your big chance to smuggle new pieces of equipment into the house past the spousal unit. That way, next spring when it shows its face in the light of day and someone asks "where did that come from," you can honestly say, "the basement!" And in moments of true cabin fever frustration, your boat equipment is there, to be fondled.

2. Every good survivalist must learn to forage for supplies. Winter is an excellent time to wisely patrol through the continuous flood of catalogues in search of the unauthorized bargain or the straggling close-out. Choose your targets carefully, fix credit cards and charge!

3. Prepare. The winter of '95 would be an excellent time to take a boating safety course. You could take a basic course if you never have done so, a refresher if its been awhile, or an advanced course to further your skills.

It could be a good time to see that the rest of your crew gets a few classroom hours under their flare gun belt too. Here's a radical suggestion, do like me: Participate in the group or organization that teaches your favorite safe boating class. Your crew can take the course, you can help the instructors with home work checking, etc. and at the same time, it serves as a refresher to you! Eventually they may even let you teach the class!

4. Plan, plan, plan! Pull out the charts. Grab some cruising guides. Start planning next summer's schedule of events! Even if you only make it halfway around your list,

just try and tell me you won't have fun "plotting" the trouble you can get into on the lake next summer.

The bottom line here is that you'll find it a lot easier to survive the season of no surf if you consider boating a year round pastime, like farming. (Like farming?!) Yes, a farmer is a farmer year round. But there is a season for planting, a season for tending and a season for harvest. There is also a season when the land rests but the farmer "repairs and prepares" for the next cycle.

Just because your boat gets shrink wrapped doesn't mean you do too. This is the season for what we call "winter cruising" in which you launch the land yacht and go in search of new harbors to discover by water next year. Take a weekend at a bed and breakfast and enjoy some travel time that way! Plan your next season now! Buy gear! Make reservations! Make repairs! Take a class! You'd better do all these things now because next summer when the boat's in the water, you won't have time!

And if all else fails, you can always spend an hour or two snuggled up on the sofa with your extra sweater and leaf through a brochure about some far away port you've put on next summer's hit list. And as you look at the nice pictures, think back to last summer when you entered some other port for the very first time. The day was oppressively muggy. The air hung like curtains in a cheap sauna. And the gnats that weren't collecting in front of your face that windless day, were sticking to your sweaty body. God, I love gnats...

The Flare

It was several years ago, shortly after Jenvey bought *Raven's Nest*. He, his oldest son and I were taking the boat on its first overnight, shakedown cruise. The weather had been deteriorating all afternoon to where we were now in what was later called a gale. We were motor-sailing, very slowly, under a reefed-down mainsail. Actually, the sail was doing us little good but it was far too rough to lower it now. We were clawing our way to the protection of the west shore of Lake St. Clair near the Grosse Point Yacht Club so that we could lower the sail in the relatively calmer waters and winds.

But along the way, we encountered a small day-sailor. The boat had capsized and there were two swimsuit- (and life-jacket-) clad crew members struggling to right the craft. The boat was small, the waves were big and the cold wind was literally against them.

We were already in contact with the Coast Guard when we came close to the overturned boat and offered them the chance to abandon ship and climb aboard. With this wind and our mainsail still partially up, we couldn't come around for a second try...this was it. They declined as they were convinced they could right their vessel and get it back to shore (they must have had a heck of a deposit on this thing). We slowly passed them by but slowed our engine RPMs to make bare minimal headway. But then the boat they were trying to right, started to break-up in the pounding waves. So, we were back on the radio and within minutes, the rescue boat was within sight. And that's where the most embarrassing moment in my life begins.

Although we were the only boat on the horizon, flying a large, white, triangular piece of Dacron...and although we were fewer than a hundred yards past the overturned daysailor and the Coast Guard rescue boat was visible in the distance...they asked us to set off a flare. Jenvey tossed me his signal kit and asked me to handle the request while he struggled with the helm in the churning seas and his son ran the radio down in the cabin.

I didn't have the heart to tell him that I had never set off a flare before. After all, I'd never been in distress let alone, out in weather like this. I opened the kit. Inside, I found a large collection of incendiary devices, and so as not to disturb him with silly questions, I selected my own weapon.

I pulled out the plastic 12-gauge flare gun that is common in those kits, quickly figured out how to insert one of those shotgun things and closed the chamber. I was confident in my choice as these things are supposed to send up a visible signal some 250 or 300 feet in the air. They've gotta see that! I pointed the pistol skyward but realized the high winds might blow the flare off course a little once it became airborne, and might make us harder to find. To compensate, I aimed the gun forward on an elevation of about forty-five degrees into the wind. In my best TV-cop impersonation, I held the gun with two hands, cocked the hammer and pulled the trigger.

From that instant, everything seemed to move in slow motion. As I pulled the trigger, I heard a voice from the helm shouting, "No!" But it was too late for "No!" The hammer hit, the flare ignited and the blazing red ball of fire exited the barrel of my trusty shootin' iron.

The flare came out of the gun...about six inches, and

immediately turned back with the wind and raced off parallel with the water like a cruise missile. It nearly parted Jenvey's hair as it exited our stern and I breathed a quick sigh of relief. It was short lived. It took me just one more slow motion instant to realize that the very people we were trying to save were directly in the path of the runaway flare. My mind did a quick calculation and judged the distance: Yes, the target was within range and there they were…watching it come directly at them.

The flare drew closer as my mind raced. What must be going through these poor guys' minds? Why were we shooting at them? How was I going to explain this to the Coast Guard? I could hear it now:

"They'll be easy to spot, Coast Guard. They're the ones that are on fire."

The flare drew even closer. Would the Court of Inquiry believe this small, day-sailor had developed an engine compartment fire? Lightning? How about spontaneous combustion?

The red missile was zeroing in on them. Smoking! That's it! The fire was caused by careless smoking! That is, if anyone would believe two drenched guys in the water, hugging a hull, managed to get their Zippos going…A light! I could say that while they didn't want to abandon ship, they did ask us for a light! Who am I to deny two shipwrecked men their last smoke? Reality set in that no one would buy these well-thought-out scenarios and I could here the eleven o'clock news in my head:

"The defendant, John Kenneth Bruce, was held without bond."

But then, as suddenly as it had turned toward the capsized boat, the flare ran out of propellant and dove into the lake fewer than ten feet from the unintended target. It hit the water hard and extinguished itself in a huge cloud of white smoke that immediately swept over the two men and the

John Kenneth Bruce

small boat. Joyously, I looked over my shoulder towards the approaching Coast Guard rescue boat. The Coastie in the bow was pointing at the capsized vessel and the Helmsman was changing course in their direction. The men would be saved and we had helped! I nonchalantly blew the smoke from my gun barrel ala' Wyatt Earp, and stuck the weapon in my belt.

Within minutes, the rescue vessel cut back behind our wake, now with two blanketed and shivering figures on board. And as they passed nearby, they tooted their horn and waved a salute...though I don't think the two additional passengers were waving with all five fingers...

All Hail, Sony…

When I was in college, my roommate's girlfriend once asked about the origin of his sophisticated stereo equipment, specifically, the name brand.

"Sony," he explained, "was the name of the ancient Japanese God of electronics." Being a city-girl and a baby-boomer who couldn't remember life before TV (I'm being kind) she accepted this explanation.

It comes back to me now, because of a tragic scenario I witnessed when visiting a friend's home marina last summer. It concerns the marketing shortcomings of the boating industry, but more directly, it's a reflection of our own shortcomings as recreational boaters. As this marina season is just getting underway, I thought it would be a good time to share it with all of you.

My friend keeps his boat in a very popular marina. One so popular, it has in fact, become quite crowded and the marina facilities have become overtaxed.

"Why would they do this?" I asked. He looked at me in mild disbelief and annoyance.

"Why, to get away from it all!" he said.

It seems the people in this marina spend all week long crowded into look-alike subdivisions, living life along the straight and narrow suburban streets…keeping between the lines, you know. Boating is their chance to get away from all that. Yet, here was an environment where those very same people stayed the whole weekend on boats thirty feet or less, tied to narrow docks in numbered slips along straight and narrow slices of seawall.

No one left the marina. It seems there were a good many reasons to choose from: Too rough, too busy, too hot, too cold, too expensive, too much work and of course my favorite; "I like it here." Say what they will, I am the casual observer type and I came to my own conclusions.

Everyone sitting in the shade, laying in a cockpit, or even snoozing in a bunk, had a retail boating catalog. Everyone! And when they finished looking at one, they would trade with their neighbors and start the browsing process all over again. And if they weren't trading catalogs, they were conferring and comparing notes over this device or that device. And what devices were they always comparing? Why, 12 volt electronic gizmos and gadgets of course!

"Did you see this new GPS?"

"How about this 12-volt toaster?"

"Maybe we should have this 12-volt VCR too!"

It went on and on, late into the night. Then, they read their catalogs by the light of 12-volt lanterns and sometimes conferred by VHF handi-talkies fresh out of the 12-volt chargers. Late night purchases were made by cell phone, complete with 12-volt adapters and one man even modemed his order in off the 12-volt, laptop computer. A lost earring was found under the picnic table with the help of a hand-held spotlight, the kind that can melt buoys at a hundred yards.

Throughout the night, I heard ice machines tinkle gently as CD players set sweet music drifting softly across the water. There was the occasional whir of a 12-volt blender as another round of drinks was mixed somewhere down the pier. Next to me, I could hear the constant sound of running water as someone's air conditioner controlled the climate of their dreams.

I think these people never left the marina, because they were addicted to shore power! I knew it long before I turned out my own lights and adjusted my own air-conditioning...and while I do love those things, I can live without them when need be. I was certain these folks could not. There were no batteries on the planet that could stand up to these abuses, without a doubt, these boats needed constant shore power to keep things whirring and tinkling. And while my friend strongly disagreed with me, my point was about to be proven.

I woke up the next morning to a strange silence. There was no rushing water, no tinkling ice machines, no whirring blenders, no blipping GPSs and no electronic voices from TV or stereo. I crawled from my bunk actually enjoying the silence when my eyes fell on the control panel next to the galley. The lights, or lack of, told the tale: There had been a power failure! I stuck my head out of the cabin and looked at the constantly lit pop machines standing next to the dollar bill changers...all were dark. The entire marina was without power. I quietly took up position in a lawn chair under the small shade tree and waited for the show to begin.

It started with a shrieking woman whose 12-volt coffee maker had gone cold. Following that came the disappointed and angry voices from those who had just discovered that this morning's homemade, country breakfast.., couldn't be microwaved. Then, men crawled out from their cockpits carrying dead handi-talkies that didn't recharge over night. After much discussion (this took time because it had to be face to face), they came to the same conclusion I had about the lack of juice in the marina.

Being a creative crowd, they attempted to correct the problem. A metal detector was used to trace the underground line to a breaker box in a dark room on the back of the pool house. Night-vision binoculars were used so that one at a time, the men of the marina could step into the darkened room and see the damage for themselves. Yes...that's what a darkened circuit box looks like all right...not that any of us could tell the difference but it sure made us feel better having had a look.

Judging from the amount of carbonized residue on and around the box, whatever had stopped the flow of juice, had been catastrophic in nature. Suggestions flew about: Power surge, lightning strike, inadequate construction, cheap parts...That's it! It was the marina operator's fault!

"My wife's electric blanket has gone cold!"

"Electric blanket?" I asked in the early July morning.

"Sure, she finds the air conditioner too cold so she plugs in her electric blanket!"

It was apparent to me the poor breaker box was not the victim of natural disaster, power company anomalies or neglect by the marina operator. The poor thing had surrendered to exhaustion. But they were bound to blame somebody.

"Wait 'til the marina operator gets here!"

"We were in the middle of a load of laundry when things went black!"

"Our dishwasher is full of cold, soapy water!"

"Wait, he's coming down the road now, I can see his van on my radar!"

And so the peasants gathered with their torches as the evil doctor returned to the castle, not realizing the monster he had created. He was seized at once as he entered the property and was swept up for trial by a kangaroo court.

Pity be his. He was found guilty of negligence and a jury of his piers (*sic*) sentenced him to death...in the electric chair. But unfortunately, no one had a 12-volt electric chair...They had toasters, blenders, stereos and radar. They had flashlights, floodlights, satnav and sonar. But no electric chairs. The called the catalog company and alas, they were

Stupid Boat Tricks

on back order. There was nothing left to do but set the man free, pack up, and go home to the straight and narrow subdivisions.

Myself, I started my engines and zoomed across the open water to sanity...with a stop at Kelleys Island and a visit to the Village Pump. There, Gary Finger poured me a famous brandy alexander and gave me a basket of onion rings. I drank, I ate, and retold this tale, doing my best to curb my natural desire for exaggeration.

You Can Always Count on the Coast Guard...

Traditionally, those who race the Mackinac are a brave and hearty sort. They are not fair weather sailors to say the least. Be there wind, snow, sleet, rain, and of course, dark of night, they are out there beating into the worst of it for the glory of it all. When they deliver those same vessels from harbor to harbor, to get ready for the next starting line, they take on this responsibility with the same dedication. They are professionals...but they are not immune from a few stupid boat tricks of their own!

It was a number of years ago when the tired racers were coming down Lake Huron on their way back from Mackinac Island. It was late and the forecast was deteriorating. They were near the tip of Michigan's thumb when they remembered hearing about a brand new marina being built in Harbor Beach. This sounded like a good excuse to call it a night and the decision was made to enter the giant breakwalls where the Coast Guard station stood watch from the center of the harbor.

But as they cleared the lighthouse at the entrance, a wall of fog and rain enveloped them. They could no longer see the bow of the good ship *Racing Vessel* and the water was dead quiet. There was the faint glow of lights briefly visible here and there, but nothing the crew of *Racing Vessel* could identify as this mysterious new marina. They crept around the spacious harbor for what seemed like hours, the navigator desperately trying to "dead reckon" their position on a harbor chart with every turn and mark.

Suddenly, the keel ground to an unexpected halt as the bow pulpit broadsided an unidentified object. Instantly, the well-trained crew leapt into action. Every member had his post to check for damage: the hull, the bilge, the engine compartment. The navigator was responsible for the VHF radio operations:

"Coast Guard, Coast Guard, this is the *Racing Vessel*. We have suffered a collision and a grounding in your harbor."

Then he unkeyed the microphone and waited for the Coasties to respond. They heard a voice answer them, but it didn't come over the radio speaker, instead it drifted over the decks, through the fog.

"Is that you?" came the voice from a second story window.

It seems the unexpected object they had hit was indeed the United States Coast Guard. In those days, the old station that stands on stilts in the harbor was still very much in use, and this crew had found it.

The vessel was secured and plans were started to free her, but not before one thoughtful Coastie brought the racing crew some coffee. It was no big deal, he later said.

"I just had to hand it to them over the rail…"

Faster Than a Speeding Bullet...

This is a stupid boat trick someone pulled me aside and told me about. I wasn't there to witness it, but then, neither was anyone but the crew of the vessel in question. This is another one of those all too true tales where we have had to change the names to protect the guilty (and our liability). Enjoy...

It was a calm Lake Huron morning when the crew of *Blowboat Deluxe* set out from Harbor Beach. They were off on a major crossing...Tobermory would be their berth tonight, after braving the open waters of Huron for the very first time. But they were ready! All the latest in navigation equipment was installed and working perfectly, including a bright and shiny new radar (a very valuable piece of equipment)!

Unfortunately, *Blowboat Deluxe* faced flat, calm waters and was motoring along at a stunning four knots instead of pounding the bounding main at perhaps a fashionable five or six. Then it happened. A soft blanket of fog (of course it wasn't in the weather forecast!) covered them. In fact, it covered them so completely that they lost sight of their own bow only thirty-seven feet away! It was a real peasouper and what a time to have it happen! They were approaching the Canadian shore complete with its shipping lanes and did I mention the Mackinac Racers? Well, it was also time for the Port Huron to Mackinac Race and somewhere out in that fog was a fleet of racing boats along with those freighters. What

Stupid Boat Tricks

a time for fog to set in! What a time to be out there! What would happen to *Blowboat Deluxe*?

The navigation instruments were running flawlessly. There was plenty of water under them, they were comfortably off shore and on course, and according to their shiny new radar (a very valuable piece of equipment!) they were alone on the horizon.

Then came the blip. It entered the radar screen from behind them and was approaching their position at a high rate of speed. The first mate of *Blowboat Deluxe* was a professional radar watcher (really, she is!) and immediately began tracking the target's range and distance.

"What an idiot!" she shouted up to her captain. "It's gotta be some super-high-speed performance boat and he's heading right for us!"

The range was now under four miles and closing, but the errant *Powerboat From Hell* had not shifted course nor altered his extremely high speed.

The captain altered course ninety degrees to get *Blowboat Deluxe* off the course of *Powerboat From Hell* and let him pass on by...hopefully, into oblivion. But no sooner had they altered course, then so did the other boat and again, they were on a collision course with the distance closing rapidly.

Again the captain took evasive action based on the guidance of his faithful mate watching the radar screen. (A very valuable piece a equipment!) But once again, *Powerboat From Hell* altered his course to match and still, collision looked immanent. Now, through the fog, they could hear the drone of the approaching engines, a signal that only seconds were left to save the crew of *Blowboat Deluxe*.

In a desperate move, the captain began sounding his aerosol-powered (yet environmentally friendly) horn in hopes that it might be heard over the deafening engines aboard *Powerboat From Hell*. He threw the helm over one last time and looked to the heavens in a last minute prayer. Like many Great Lakes fogs, they may be thick, but they are often only a few feet high.

While the captain couldn't see the bow of *Blowboat Deluxe*, he could indeed see the masthead and vague, whisps of blue sky above. He had time to squeeze out his quick prayer, a confession or two and several life-style altering promises before *Powerboat From Hell* was on top of them.., literally. Coaching shouts from first mate had ceased. She must be praying too...Then, he thought he could hear her crying.

As the last word of the last promise rolled off the captain's lips, the roar reached its zenith and as he looked towards the heavens, a small Cessna aircraft shot over the masthead and passed them on its way to the Canadian shore, taking it's engine sound with it.

The captain sat limp at the helm. It was then he realized the crying noises from below were really gasps of laughter. The first mate, a professional air-traffic controller, had finally figured out her target was an aircraft moments before the encounter and was laughing too hard to tell the captain that all those promises to the deity...were really not needed. It seems their masthead was protruding up from the fog layer much like a shark's fin above the surface. The curious airplane was following them!

And what of the captain? He has actually kept some of the life-style altering promises, some of the time...

"It Was Quicker This Way…"

The funny thing about stupid boat tricks is that when you tell one, you will soon hear several more. They're contagious. This one comes to us clandestinely from an experienced marine patrol officer who works the open shore near a large, urban area. Due to the nature of his employment and the crime against boating committed here, we have had to once again change the names to protect the guilty.

We shall refer to our guardian of the waterways as Officer X, his rookie sidekick, fresh from inland lake duty, experiencing his first day of big boat duty, we shall call Officer Y. And the star of our show, the man of the hour, the one who really makes this boat trick stupid…shall be known as Lotto-Boy.

It was a hot, lazy, summer afternoon on the big water. Officer X was showing Officer Y the ropes of the "big boat duty." In fact, he had spent most of the shift trying to impress upon, or simply impress, his young associate as to just how different it was out here.

"There's a whole lot more to this out here than just going counter-clockwise, you know…These aren't just dime-a-dozen ski boats out here…Serious boats, serious problems, it's a whole different class of things…"

About the time the rookie was overly impressed, it happened. In the distance, about a mile and a half from shore, they could see a performance speed boat in some obvious form of distress. They could hear the engines revving and whining wildly. Great clouds of spray and exhaust shot skyward but the boat seemed unable to move. They raced towards the position to see if they could be of assistance as they radioed their encounter to the dispatcher.

As they approached, Officer Y kept a close eye on the craft through the binoculars and as they drew closer, his jaw dropped in disbelief. He handed the binoculars to Officer X with nothing said. Officer X steadied the glasses the best he could and viewed the approaching target. He took a long hard look as the rookie took the helm. In amazement, he put the glasses down as he still stared, dumbfounded at the distressed vessel.

"I guess you were right about a different class of boaters..." said Officer Y as they pulled up along side the other craft.

Officer X was maintaining his composure as much as his flushed faced would allow him to conceal.

"Good afternoon, sir..." he addressed the sole occupant of the speedboat. "Brand new boat?"

"Well, yeah..." answered the studly young man at the controls.

He was obviously embarrassed and frustrated that the afternoon was not going as he had anticipated.

"I see you haven't even put any registration numbers or license on the hull yet," said Officer X.

In the conversation that followed, it came out that the young man had hit the weekly Lotto just a few days before and had dashed down to the dealer to buy this boat (hence the name, Lotto-Boy). He had picked up the boat and trailer at the dealership just a couple of hours ago and had immediately brought his new pride and joy to the public ramps.

"But the dealer told me this boat could do 70 miles an hour..." puzzled Lotto-Boy. "And I haven't be able to get 'er over 15 yet!"

"I see," said Officer X as they slowly circled the craft. "Maybe if you had left the trailer back on shore..."

Yes! It was clearly evident to the officers from some distance away what all the smoking and spraying was all about. There, still firmly attached under the boat, here, a mile-and-a-half from the ramp...Lotto-Boy still had his new boat trailer with him! It was suspended there by the two heavy-duty straps at the stern and the firmly-tightened winch cable.

"Ya know..." said Lotto-Boy in his moment of realization, "I saw those other trucks and trailers in the parking lot and I wondered about that...but it was so much quicker to launch it this way..."

Doing their best to contain themselves, the officers set about the business of helping Lotto-Boy shut down his now overheated engines and contacting the dispatcher to arrange for a commercial tow. With no insurance, Lotto Boy was about to learn a very expensive lesson. But one more comment from the dispatcher is worth our attention.

"Is the vessel towable as is, or will special equipment be needed?" came the voice over the radio.

And while looking Officer X directly in the eye, Officer Y smugly said:

"No, he's ready to be towed all the way home. In fact, this is the most completely equipped vessel I have ever seen...inland or off-shore..."

The two officers have never discussed this event between them again.

Rub-A-Dub-Dub...

This is a really stupid boat trick, and honestly, one that could have very easily, ended in tragedy. While we may find humor in this tale, let it also serve to remind us of the unnecessary dangers and risks we sometimes bring upon ourselves and others. It's stupid, let's laugh and hopefully, never see this again. There is no need to change the names here, because I never knew their names, but it was a night I will remember for a long time.

I was quietly sitting on the back deck of my Sea Ray 30, *Moonraker*, at the state harbor on Beaver Island. It was late, but a beautiful moonlit night and the wife and I were enjoying the calm of the harbor after having sentenced the small ones to bed for the night. I could see the shadows of other folks in other cockpits around the marina enjoying the night as well.

All was peaceful, all was calm, when the night was suddenly shattered by the shrill, screeching laughter of a woman. There, coming down the road from the famed Shamrock Bar, were the staggering images of four people, two men and two women who obviously had far more than just a snoot-full. They were loud and raucous as they approached the docks...especially that one woman. She seemed to find everything hysterically funny and that laugh of hers...well, the entire marina knew she was coming.

Stupid Boat Tricks

Don't get me wrong. I don't deny anyone a good time and I know there have been moments in my own past when I was a bit on the loud and loose side. No, I was not offended by these people's behavior as I knew they would soon find a bunk and sleep it off. Actually, I, and several other of the shadow people in the marina, watched in amusement. Hey, this was cheap entertainment.

Down the dock came the four revelers. We all watched to see which of the lucky boats they would call home. But to our surprise, and shock, they selected not one of the comfortable cruising yachts safely secured in one of the slips, but a small, hard-shell dinghy with an outboard motor, tied up to the old ladder at one end of the pier. They were from the large sailboat anchored out in the bay and somehow, in this condition, they were going to get back out there!

Now my attention was focused on the effort just a few feet away. I sensed everyone else was watching this show with keen interest too. I had a couple of life jackets at the ready, just in case. Down into the dinghy (it was just a couple of ladder steps) climbed first one, then another, each performing their own brand of alcoholic-acrobatics as they moved from the stable dock, down the flimsy ladder and into the very tender little dinghy. This was also great entertainment for the woman with the shrill laugh who was the last to make the great attempt herself.

When it finally came her turn, she seemed to have great difficulty comprehending the function of the ladder. She approached it one way, then another, and then yet again from the opposite side. This simple task had baffled her and she found it all, hysterically amusing. Finally, the man who I assumed was her husband, lost patience and shouted at her.

"Forget the %$&*(%@ ladder and just step into the %&$*@$# boat!"

Not one to argue with her husband, she saluted and

obeyed...stepping off into space and suddenly finding the cold waters of St. James Bay literally around her. The high, shrieky laughter was silenced and replaced by much sputtering and obscenity calling. Those who say there is nothing madder than a wet hornet, have not heard the wrath of a drenched drunk.

I was ready to fling my life jackets in her direction, but they quickly seemed to have everything reasonably under control. Soon, she, and half the bay, were crawling up the ladder, and then falling back into the little dinghy. But the loud and wet woman was now even offensive to her shipmates. No one wanted to sit next to her, she was dripping on all of them!

They wanted her to sit by herself on the bow seat. She refused. She shook her arms in anger and discomfort. Everybody got wetter. The other couple moved to the bow seat to escape her, let her husband suffer the displeasure! But he wanted no part of her either in this condition. Again she refused to move her seat. So he did the only thing he could think of in his condition...he joined the other couple, crunched up on the bow seat leaving her alone at the back of the boat...and in control of the outboard motor!

The very instant it became obvious that this woman was going to command this dinghy, everyone of us shadow people seemed to spring to life and took position to defend our hulls. Now, our life jackets were replaced by a far more practical tool, the ever-popular boat hook. I looked up and down the canal at the spiny sight of all those boat hooks...it looked like a casting call for *Moby Dick*.

With one disgusted pull, the drenched and sputtering woman started the small outboard as they pushed off from the pier. She flipped the lever into forward and twisted that handle to full throttle. But there's one thing this intoxicated crew had not planned on, had not foreseen, had not thought through: With all those people in the bow, the dinghy was obviously a little nose-down in the water. With the sudden thrust of the outboard, the dinghy didn't jump up on the waves and skitter across the surface...it dove like a submarine!

What must have seemed like a massive wave of water piled over the bow and drenched the entire crew. In fact, the only thing that stayed dry in that boat, was the dependable little outboard that continued to putter away. The dinghy, obviously filled with positive flotation, surfaced, as far as the gunwales and there they all sat...four drunks in a gas-powered bath tub.

The helmsman found this terribly entertaining again and the shrieking laughter returned. Now, filled with water, the best this little boat could do was a harmless knot or so and that's how they plowed through the water...up one set of docks and down the other trying to find their way to the open bay and back to their boat. I think she knew where the opening was...I think she was just taking the rest of her crew on a little midnight harbor tour for the entire marina to enjoy. They eventually found their boat and tied up with a good "thump." We could still hear the shrieking laughter as they stripped-off the dripping clothes in the cockpit before finding the warmth of the cabin. And then there was silence...

The Day It Hit the Fan...

This story starts with a dream, and ends with a nightmare. As is often the case, we have changed the names to protect the guilty...and our butts.

Mr. & Mrs. Trawler had finally decided to give up sailing and get into one of those comfortable, slow-going displacement-type vessels. After a long search, the good ship *Slow-Motion* was found. She was an aging ship, a 40+ foot trawler, in wood, powered by two powerful four-cylinder diesels. Feeding these thrifty powerhouses under the floorboards were four separate steel fuel tanks of about 75 gallons each.

Steel tanks, did he say? But Steel Rusts! No, these tanks are filled with diesel fuel and what's diesel fuel? Oil! The tanks are constantly oiled and rust is not a problem (at least that was the thinking at the time of manufacture).

As time passed, Mr. & Mrs. Trawler enjoyed their boat immensely, but realized they just weren't traveling on it as much as they had hoped. In fact, except for the trip in and out of winter storage, a 25-mile jaunt across open Lake St. Clair, the good ship *Slow-Motion* spent most of it's time tied to the dock and was used as a weekend cottage. The four, 75-gallon fuel tanks seemed like such a waste and unfortunately, the 6-gallon holding tank for the head now seemed inadequately small.

After several years of frequent trips to the pumpout, Mr.

Trawler suffered a stroke of presumed genius: If he could convert one of the four fuel tanks to use as an additional holding tank...his problems would be solved!

Wait...he said those were steel tanks. And it won't be filled with oil anymore...it will be filled with a substance, primarily water but also containing caustic chemicals and, well, some really nasty stuff!

Mr. Trawler did the re-plumbing job himself and all seemed well. But by the spring of the following year, he noticed a slight dripping coming from that converted tank in the bilge. The welds on the seams looked a little red too, so he painted the tank. The paint smell helped kill the other smell that seemed to never go away now. Their friends expressed concern for the tank.

But by the end of the season, the mysterious dripping has ceased! All was well again!

"See, I told ya!" proudly said the Trawlers...and life went on...for another three years.

But wait! Any science student knows that the dripping stopped because sediment probably settled into the holes! That tank is still rusting from the inside out! Good Lord, it's a time bomb waiting to go off!

Frederick Stonehouse, the famous shipwreck author, is a friend of mine. He once told me, "You know, it seems most good shipwreck stories start out with, 'It was the last trip of the season'..."

To which I answered: "That's ironic, most good stupid boat tricks start off with, 'It was the first trip of the year'..."

I think you know what's going to happen. But ask yourselves, is this going to happen while calmly sitting at the dock? How about while motoring around the canals or over to the pumpout? How about, three miles off shore with heavy seas on the bow?

It was the first trip of the year. Mr. & Mrs. Trawler were taking the good ship *Slow-Motion* from winter storage to their home port, across open Lake St. Clair. But you know about those spring storms. The winds were blowing a good thirty or so and the shallow lake was kicking up to nice five-footers off-shore. It was cold too and the couple was down below in the cozy cabin steering from the lower station. And then it happened.

You can call it what you want...all hell broke loose, IT hit the fan...choose your favorite phrase but in any event, it began with a crashing noise below. Within seconds, the bilge pump started to blow. There was...that old familiar odor. In a panic, Mr. Trawler handed the helm to Mrs. Trawler and he grabbed the handle on the hatch in the floor boards that would give him access to the engine compartment. He pulled it open.

Funny thing about diesel engines, water won't douse 'em the way it can a gasoline engine. In fact, as long as they have their air intakes clear, many of "em can run under water! They just run and run and run...

As the hatch opened, Mr. Trawler immediately realized what had happened. In a hurry last fall, he had not pumped this converted tank dry. There were now about fifty or so gallons of...extraneous fluid...surging around in the engine compartment, covering and coating everything. This included the fan belts on the engines which were now in the business of freely distributing the extraneous fluid at high speeds and low angles. Since the hatch was open, it was now being freely distributed about the interior of the cabin too. Fortunately, Mr. Trawler was standing behind the open hatch and it protected him like a shield. Unfortunately, Mrs. Trawler was at the helm and received much of the distribution.

Amongst the swearing, the screaming and the death threats, the bilge pump was killed, for ecological reasons, and the hatch was quickly closed. It became necessary to weigh it down with the spare anchor and other gear to stem

Stupid Boat Tricks

the tide against the surging liquid. Even so, a good amount of it oozed into the cabin and permeated the rest of the good ship *Slow-Motion*. They were still nearly two hours from port...

Upon their arrival, no announcement was needed. The boat was pumped, the hull hoisted and the entire craft cleaned, sanitized, purified, fumigated and then listed for sale. It has been several years now. Anybody want a deal?

Look Who's Driving!

My wife and I passed a milestone in our lives last month. My fifteen-year-old daughter got her learner's permit. That's right. She's driving the family Land Yacht now.

Normally, this is a time of great anxiety for many parents. The child who just this morning couldn't be responsible for finding her own clothes or making her own bed, now wants you to hand her the keys to one of Detroit's own motor machines...your motor machine! If that weren't enough, for the next several months you are expected to go along for the ride and sit up front...right up close and personal in full view of everything whizzing by. It's a panicking thought, isn't it?

Of course, as soon as they are behind the wheel, they think they are in control of everything, like the stereo and air conditioning too. That's probably your own fault though. When they were younger and wanted to change these things, you didn't tell them the truth. Rather than say "you can't change it because we are selfish, self-centered dictators who don't care about your taste in music or climate control preferences," you copped-out by saying "I'm the driver and I control those things..."

A little more than a decade later it comes back to bite you in the buns because now...they are the drivers and they expect to control those things. You may get to avoid some of it by proclaiming a controlled driving environment," but for the most part, you are about to have your musical horizons expanded while suffering an extreme in temperatures. All this and you haven't even left the driveway yet.

You'll notice I'm using the "you" here and not the "I." That's because I saw this coming years ago and have taken steps to prepare myself. First of all, I had no qualms about telling my children that I was a selfish dictator and I controlled the radio and the climate control by divine right. Go ahead, ask 'em. But in addition to this frankness, I also entrusted them with ever-increasing amounts of responsibility starting at very young ages. As boaters, this was easy and the means were directly at hand.

When my kids were much younger, they were allowed to take the dinghy out and about the marina. They never realized we, or our spies, were keeping very careful tabs on them from the end of every dock and occasionally coordinating our efforts via VHF radio. But they learned how to row, they learned responsibility for their actions (supervision is the most important aspect here), and they learned the importance of the buddy system. Later, when they were both older, the dinghy grew a motor and with DNR permits in hand, their boundaries expanded.

At the same time, they started taking turns at the helm of the big boat. By the time she was fourteen, my daughter was docking the boat and performing some gas dock maneuvers. Don't get me wrong. She was by no means a pro. She made mistakes and bumped a few pilings. But she was as good as many of the skippers in our marina and better than some. My wife elected to stay below during these exercises and in retrospect, that was a mistake.., more on that in a minute.

So when it became time for my daughter to get behind the wheel of the car, I had no anxiety. But here's where I have to get off my "holier than thou" soap box because while I entered the situation with no anxiety, I was the one who got

John Kenneth Bruce

educated that day!

After starting the car, adjusting the mirrors and putting it into gear, we started to back down the driveway. At the very instant we moved, a great noise came from my wife in the back seat. It was the hissing noise of rapidly inhaled air screaming between her teeth on it's way deep within her body. This was followed by a silence that held everyone's anticipation. Either she was biting her tongue or she was smoking some illicit substance back there.

We continued on. At every new experience—the first stop sign, the first freeway merge, the first boulevard crossing—my wife would take yet another hit from her imaginary joint. I was so distracted by this I nearly missed what the sweet young thing behind the wheel was doing.

She stopped short at a yellow light, surprising the man behind her who wanted to go for it. He honked his horn and threw up his arms in an irritated manner. Without hesitating, she returned the salute in the rear view mirror, although she did use all five fingers.

"Where'd you get that!?" I asked her.

"That's what you do, Daddy," she answered sweetly.

And before I could recover from the exposure of my own excess, she accidentally cut off a man in a pick-up truck who pulled up beside her at the next light. He was obviously irritated. (Isn't driving in the city, fun?) I was about to make an apologetic motion and point to the inexperienced driver when she said, "Please, Daddy..." and smiled at the driver sweetly and innocently as if nothing had happened. He was immediately disarmed.

"And where do you get off pulling that?" I asked.

"It works for mom..." was her answer. At this point, my wife took yet another hit off her joint and I was about to ask her to share as we pulled away from the light.

I guess the moral of the story here is one I'm really not too proud of: No matter how careful, insightful, instructive

Stupid Boat Tricks

and supportive we can be with our kids, they're watching us all the time. At home, in the car and on the water. Let's be careful what we teach them...

Dilbert Groggins and the Crime of the Century

For a very long time, my father has kept his boat in a sleepy little marina a distance north of Chicago along the Wisconsin shore. He enjoyed the small town atmosphere and the down-home, family flavor of the marina. Everybody knew everyone and everyone was at ease. If you packed up and left at the end of the weekend and accidentally left something of value out on your picnic table, it would surely still be there waiting for you next Friday. This was a fairly secluded marina and people would literally leave their boats without locking their doors and hatches. And then, one day, all that changed.

It was in the spring, about six years ago. Many of the marina residents were out at their boats, up in the cradles and down in the hulls getting their boats ready for launching. Dilbert Groggins was there too. Dil kept his boat in the next cut over from my father's boat, just across the narrow, gravel parking lot. What made this day different, what changed life in the marina forever, was that this was the day that Dil's car was stolen right out from under his nose!

He came up from the cabin and was getting ready to climb down the ladder to get some more tools he needed to finish the project he had been working on so diligently. But when he looked down at the base of the ladder, his aging but trusty automobile was gone...along with half his tools, a brand new bilge pump and several other items of various

Stupid Boat Tricks

values. He was dumbstruck. It had happened in a marina full of people working on their boats and no one had seen it. Professional crime had come to their marina!

To make a long story short, the police were called, a report was made but the car was never found. While the insurance company replaced the value of the car, Dil took a beating on the contents. He and the marina would never be the same again.

Over the course of that season, my father watched life change among his friends. Locks became an every day way of life. There were padlocks, combination locks, chain locks, and deadbolts where there had been nothing before. People actually took to chaining their boats to the docks, and some even chained the docks to the sea wall. Things were never left laying around anymore and whenever something came up missing, it was now assumed it had been stolen.

"Where else could it be? I left it right here and now it's gone forever..." Even if some of these items eventually turned up, it was believed they were later discarded by whomever had stolen them. Thieves were running rampant in the marina.

Upon occasion, the police were summoned to report a rash of missing items, each in its own right of little value, but when combined with this, that and the other thing, indicated a major crime trend in the area, obviously organized in Chicago and coming up this way. Drug dealers were spotted too. Mostly, they turned out to be youthful hangabouts with time on their hands, but it's better to be safe than sorry.

Over the years, as technology advanced, locks were not good enough and alarms were added; alarms with wireless beepers that would alert you to thievery and violation as it happened, in realtime, right now! I remember my father's dismay as one of his closer friends showed him the glory of his new onboard security system and when, during the course of demonstration, it became necessary to enter the disarm code, this man made my father turn his back..."just a precaution, you know." This was the same man who had often borrowed my father's car to run to the store for ice. The same man who had always told my father that if he ever needed to borrow a couple of life jackets for a family afternoon, his were under the starboard bunk. And now he made my father turn his back to keep his precious code a secret. Mutual distrust among friends and especially strangers was the order of the day.

Whatever the motivation, the measures did seem to be effective. Other than Dil's car, there was never one other single recorded significant crime. No other cars were ever stolen, no boats were ever broken into, no dinghies were ever pilfered and no outboards were ever lifted. Yes sir, the high-tech alarms had kept the rampant crime wave down to a couple of lost fishing nets (one of which turned up at home), the occasional bottle of propane and once, there was a stolen life jacket. That's a pretty efficient record all right! But whatever injustices these people had suffered over the previous five years, it was all about to change again.

It was a bright fall afternoon and my father was working

on his boat getting it ready for winter haul-out. The lake levels drop in the fall anyway, but the water in the marina was especially low that day due to the storm surge that had taken a good amount of the water over to the Michigan shore the day before. In the slip next to him, the young couple with the fancy racing sailboat was getting ready to leave their slip for the annual trip to drop the mast. They cast off lines, put the engine in reverse and backed out no more than a foot when, THUNK, they were aground. They could move forward to the sea wall but no further back than before, The low water level had caused them to hit some object with their deep keel that they had never known was there.

The guy at the end of the cut was a recreational diver and soon he was suited up and diving into the murky waters to see if he could help free the trapped sailboat. But within a couple of minutes, he shot back to the surface, tore off his mask and with no color in his face, gasped out: "Call the police! Someone's ditched a car down here and there's a body in it!"

The police were called. EMS too, to at least haul away the corpse of the poor unfortunate one inside. Word spread like fire around the marina: "Chicago gangsters had sent someone to 'sleep with the fishes,' our fishes!" Stand by, get your camera, gruesome remains to be hoisted up soon!

The sailboat was lightened by emptying the tanks and removing all the gear. It was just enough so the keel could clear the roof of the car. The local police called the State Police. The crime lab showed up and someone said the TV news was sending a chopper. But the police wouldn't wait. As soon as the giant wrecker was on the site, their own divers (this is a job for professionals) hooked the cables to the hidden hulk and ever so slowly, it was hoisted out of the muddy, murky bottom and into the marina lot.

It was green...fuzzy green. It had been down there a long time. Cameras snapped and flashed. As the weeds and larger clumps of muck fell from the car, it took on a more identifiable shape. A Plymouth...odd, most Chicago gangsters drive flashier cars than this. But wait! The license plate was still in place! This might be an easier crime to solve than they had thought. But as the crime lab boys brushed away the mud over the plate, some very outdated colors came into view.

"This one's been down there a while," said a lieutenant detective with the State Police. "Has the organized crime unit been called?"

The crime lab boys worked over the car's exterior, peeling back the mud and the algae, the weeds and the refuse...until suddenly, the wreck became very familiar. Dilbert Groggins recognized it first.

"My car!" he sputtered. "That's my car!"

"Good Lord!" thought everyone. It seems Chicago gangsters had stolen Dil's car and used it to ditch a body, right here in our own marina!

"The body! The body!" the crowd demanded and with that, the crime lab boys opened the rear door of the long-lost sedan.

Out with the remaining water washed a large, partially decomposed roll of carpeting. Dil had planned to use this "body" to pad the pilings in his slip all those years ago. The confused crowd fell silent, but no one was more silent than Dilbert Groggins for he now knew what the crime lab boys were in the process of figuring out.

After a few moments with the car and some time spent with a tape measure, the announcement was made: Dilbert Groggins' car had never been stolen. On that fateful day, five-and-a-half years ago, he had pulled up next to his boat and accidentally left the car in neutral. While he was below decks, gravity, the wind and whatever other forces could come to bear, had set the vehicle rolling. It rolled down the slight incline of the narrow, gravel parking lot, between two

Stupid Boat Tricks

cradled boats and over the seawall into a then unoccupied slip, where it sank. A marina full of people and no one saw it!

There had never been a car theft, a great crime wave or a rash of thefts. Nothing had really changed that day so long ago and there was really no reason for the padlocks, the combination locks, the chain locks and the deadbolts. All the alarms were without reason. All the isolation and alienation was for nothing. The crime of the century had never happened.

It only goes to show: If you look hard enough, you can find the bad in everyone...

The Finer Art of Anchoring

For weeks now I have patiently watched as Miller and Kaplan have dragged two fine examples of technically advanced anchors around the confines of the bay. They have measured, dropped, yanked, pulled, bobbed and hoisted these poor pieces of galvanized iron in every effort to evaluate them for upcoming articles in this very magazine. I find their efforts amusing. Don't they know that anchoring is not a science, but a well defined and practiced art?

The accomplished anchorer is one who can select his ground tackle like Rembrandt would select his colors. He can cast his anchor across the bottom with the best of the Grand Masters and do so without looking like one of Picasso's people. And as is true with any art, procedure is everything.

There are two schools of thought on the art of anchoring procedure. The first is the "I'd better do it myself" school in which the captain of his vessel takes all responsibility and action himself. This relieves all members of his crew from gaining any hands-on nautical experience above the requirement of breathing. This will also add interest and intrigue to the anchoring experience because the captain can't be at the helm and the bow at the same time. Anchoring critics will add points for the greater distance between the helm and the bow the captain must traverse so skippers of bigger boats

Stupid Boat Tricks

will have an inherent advantage.

The other school is built around the "I'll bet I can get her to do it" technique. Here, the captain engages in the anchoring process much as before, but now by remote control. He never leaves the helm, but instead sends his first mate (but certainly not his last) forward with conflicting directions which he will supplement throughout the process. His anchoring experience is further enhanced by the number of commands he can issue, multiplied by the distance between him and his current mate.

There are a few rules to follow if you want to maximize your self expression under either school of anchoring:

1. When you go forward to lower or raise your anchor, make it perfectly clear to your crew that you have left no one in particular in charge. Phrases like, "Someone take the helm" will do this quite nicely.

2. Even though all the boating safety books say you should lower, never throw your anchor, a well flung Danforth says much about the flinger. Do make certain your boat has ceased all forward motion before heaving, and then gain extra favor with the critics for hitting one or more of the following: a) A fishing boat. b) A jet ski. c) Another cruising vessel. d) An island. If any of these things are moving at the time, score double, especially the island. You can qualify as an instant Grand Master of Anchoring if you can fling your anchor into water too shallow for you to recover it.

3. Some anchoring critics will tell you that "the way you fling is everything." Undoubtedly, grace and form are important attributes. You can tell by the number of people who will pause in their own recreation and patiently watch (from a respectable distance) as a true Grand Master defines his art. There seem to be two prevalent styles, the "swinger" who swings his anchor in ever increasing arcs until it manages to strike the hull behind him. This tells him he now has sufficient momentum to "release and kerplunk." The other

style is that of the "bowler" who takes a premeasured step or two across the deck and releases in an underhand arc. Frequently, practitioners of this form will excitedly dive in after their anchors in an impatient effort to view the fruits of their own skill.

4. Once you have secured your anchor to the bottom, the work of the True Master has only begun. There are two methods you can use to dazzle your anchorage mates. One is the "magical expanding rode" in which a partially cleated anchor rode slowly plays out an increasing amount of scope. This will allow you to view the harbor from different vantage points as well as meet new and exited people, close up and personal. The alternative method is also good for this same purpose and it's really your choice as to which one to use. The "vertical rode" is accomplished by playing out a very small amount of anchor line allowing you to pound your anchor in to a plowshare and farm furrows across the bay.

5. Anchor recovery really is the "make or break" finishing touch of the Grand Master. Of course, you realize it makes no difference whether or not you actually do recover the anchor. After all, some of the most famous artists left brush bristles in their paintings. Its the valor with which you try that sets you apart in a common anchorage. The more people you can involve in hauling on the rode of a stuck anchor, the better. If you can manage to leave the helm entirely unattended in the process, you are demonstrating first class skills of an indescribable nature. Leave your engines running during this process for added bonus points.

6. Should your efforts result in the actual recovery of an anchor (yours or someone else's), you can score high marks with the post impressionists by decoratively applying mud and weed to your deck and rails via your feet and backside. This is actually easier than it sounds.

Seriously, I can tell you that at one time or other, I have

Stupid Boat Tricks

committed all the above mentioned sins. Anchoring is perhaps one of the most ignored of the basic boating skills, yet time and time again, it has proven itself to be one of the most important.

An anchor can work as a book mark in your day trip, holding your place while you enjoy lunch or a swim. It can tuck you in for the night in the solitude of an undiscovered anchorage. It can be the life line that keeps you from drifting into danger when equipment fails or Mother Nature disrupts your plans. Anchoring is serious business. Select yours carefully and don't be afraid to let someone else on board be the anchoring expert. Many famous cruising couples have divided the major duties right along the anchor line. You really can anchor "by the book" and when Miller and Kaplan have finished dragging theirs around the bay, I'm certain they'll give you food for some serious thought...

The All-Seeing Oz...

Meet Ozzie. Ozzie is one of Jenvey's friends. And like Jenvey, Ozzie loves his boat and his gadgets. In fact, the best kind of gadgetry is that which goes on the boat! Also like Jenvey, Ozzie bought his current boat with virtually no optional equipment on board so that he could have the pleasure of selecting it and installing it himself. Like the boat, much of the equipment was used and bargain followed bargain and windfall became hardware and...well...things evolved without much of a plan. But I'm getting ahead of myself here.

She was a beautiful, aging trawler the previous owner had been financially unable to hold on to. Even though she was branded with the stigma of being a "repo," her survey proved her to be sound of engine and hull. She had a spacious, enclosed pilothouse with a large flat space forward of the wheel. This space not only held a chart table, but had plenty of room for whatever other necessary pieces of equipment her captain might desire. But alas, she had no electronics. Where there were once sounders, speeders and other indicators, now there were only empty screw holes and clipped wiring.

But that was the best part for Ozzie! In short order, there was a top-of-the-line VHF mounted on that spacious dash. Then followed the new depth sounder. Being a purist, Ozzie purchased separate depth, speed, temperature and other

Stupid Boat Tricks

such indicators...and mounted them all on the dash.

By the second season, he had added redundant, digital engine instrumentation, a paper charting depth sounder in addition to the digital unit he had installed the year before and a whole row of indicators for his tanks: water, waste and both fuel tanks. And I guess I forgot to tell you about navigation equipment. There was an old LORAN, a brand new GPS, then came the digitized chartboard and then, that was followed by the LCD screen chart reader, the kind that takes those chart cartridges.

The long and the short of it is that by the end of the second season, Ozzie's dash was pretty-well crowded with a whole lot of electronics. And to make space for more, some of the smaller units were getting stacked on top of some of the others! It was getting crowded up there.

But Ozzie loved it. Shortly after he added that huge old boat anchor of a radar unit, someone in the marina had dubbed him "the all powerful, all seeing OZ." And that was OK with Ozzie too. He rather liked the wizard-like nickname and enjoyed the attention his collection of electronics would bring. Whenever there was a storm, a crowd would form in his pilothouse to watch it sweep across the radar screen, to track it on the interfaced chart reader and to watch the weather station digitally record the rainfall, wind speed and temperature drop.

Ozzie was the guy who would always interfere with your TV because he was running everything from radar to wind chill indicator while tied to the dock. There were jokes, envious jokes for the most part, about Ozzie's jet cockpit, and about how he had an instrument rating for his "landings." People would ask him how he could see around all that stuff and the pat answer was "with this much stuff, I don't need to! I can feel my way in the dark!"

Well, all good things must come to an end. And so ended Ozzie's reign as the "all seeing Oz." It didn't come on some dark and stormy night while miles from home. It didn't come during a fierce gale that ripped at the ship's very existence. It came on a calm, sunny afternoon in his own marina and at the hands of his own dinghy.

Ozzie had a small, hard-shell dinghy with a small outboard he carried on the back deck of the trawler. That is, when he was traveling. Often on weekends in the marina, he would just leave the dinghy tied in his slip while he took the big boat out for an afternoon ride. And on this fateful day, that's exactly what he did.

However, on this day, he didn't tie the dinghy as closely to the dock pilings as he could have, which allowed it to drift out into the main part of the boat slip. This made what is normally a very close fit, impossible. Then in came the "all seeing Oz" down the canal with his radar spinning and his sounders beeping and the rest of his electronic menagerie doing whatever it is they did.

The rest of the marina watched in shock as Ozzie turned the heavy trawler into his slip only to collide with the dinghy. At the first sounds of rending fiberglass, he threw the vessel into full reverse, but trawlers stop about as quickly as freight trains. There was a terrible crunching and grinding and when it was over, the poor dinghy was in pieces and resting on the bottom of the slip.

What had happened? With all that modern high-tech, electronic boat gear on the dashboard of that boat, the "all seeing Oz" could not see over the top of it all. He never saw the dinghy…until he crawled down to the dock in shame and looked at it below the surface of the water.

Practice Makes Perfect

Last summer, while on vacation, I had the opportunity to see two examples from the opposite extremes in the realm of docking expertise. It was a fairly good-sized transient harbor in the heart of a small Great Lakes town. While a number of locals and hearty commuters keep their boats there for the season, a majority of the dock space is rented out a day or two at a time.

There I was, relaxing on the fan tail of *Moonraker* when the snappy couple just two boats down decided to get underway. While the engine was warming, he undid the deftly-tied cleat hitches, took one turn around the cleat and returned the balance of the line aboard to his wife. She held the minimum number of lines needed to keep them in the slip while the others were removed. Once behind the wheel, he gave a well-rehearsed cue and snap! The lines were loosed, the outdrive kicked into gear and they were smoothly away from the dock…poetry in motion.

About an hour later, a young family on a 27-foot fishing boat decided to go trolling for the afternoon. Their undocking experience was a little different. A steady breeze was coming in over the breakwall and where they were tied, it was hitting them bow-on. Like the first couple, he warmed the engine while he tended his dock lines, but there, all similarity ended.

John Kenneth Bruce

He had tied his dock lines (some of which were clothesline, some of which were polypropylene) yes, he had tied them to the dock cleats in large, multiple, mega-knots. I assumed he might be staying for a while…like into the millennium. But to his credit, he wasn't trying to untie these Gordian knots, he was merely slipping the loops at the other end of the lines, off of his deck cleats.

Of course, as he released each line, from the bow towards the stern, the boat was caught by the wind and swung out of the slip. There was no boat next to him and no fourth tie point, so he could swing from the stern, a full 180 degrees. And that's just what he did. When he had unhooked the last line, there he stood, at the end of the dock, one arm wrapped around the piling and the other hand holding tightly to the stern rail of the boat. The boat itself now stretched across the canal, dangerously close the other boats on the next dock. On board, his wife and two children (about 7- and 10-years-old) watched as the engine idled.

This was a fine mess, I thought. What does he do now? Well, he had a plan! He got his wife to crawl off the back of the swim platform and gently take his place as "Atlas," holding the boat and the dock together. I must admit, my heart stopped as the two children, alone on the running boat, started to look at the steering wheel and shifter…but then decided to leave it alone.

Meanwhile, as she held the boat, he ran up and down the dock, now untying his horrendous, knotted creations and collecting his docklines! Now, while he did this in a surprisingly short time, you could tell by the wince on his wife's face that he had about maxed-out his time when he finally came to her relief. Then, she climbed back over the swim platform and into the helm position. On his cue, he stepped off the dock, onto the platform, hanging onto the stern rail as she threw it into gear and gave it a shot of throttle in a hard, right turn.

Miraculously, she missed the other boats on the next dock. Her husband was not thrown into the prop wash, vegematic-style. Her children didn't try to help. And as they puttered past me, out of the marina, he climbed over the rail himself and gently took his place at the helm.

I thought about this for a while, thinking I have never seen such a classic example of Laurel & Hardy seamanship in my life...thinking how lucky they were to have actually pulled this maneuver off, when it hit me: They only way they could have pulled this maneuver off is to have practiced it again and again. That's when I realized this couple, as unorthodox as they appeared, were just as well-rehearsed as the first couple. This is the way they always do it!

"Insane," said my wife when I told her of my theory.

But I was proven right. That evening, the boat returned and tied up again, in the same manner, in the same slip (musta been afraid someone would steal those dock lines). The next morning, we again watched a repeat performance of the very same un-docking procedure. They had it down pat! At the end of the day, they took the boat over to the launch ramp (a story I shall save for another time) retrieved their patient vessel and trailered home for the week.

It was only as they hauled the boat from the water that I actually noticed the name on the transom: *Synergy* whereby all things come together in their own harmony...

Navigation: The Winter Rules

I used to play golf. Don't worry, it was a long time ago. In fact I think it was in a previous life. But it's a silly game whenever you play it. You lug a large bag of equipment around on a hot day, hit a little white ball as far away as you can, and then go and try to find it. If you find it, you hit it away again. If you're good at this, you might do it a hundred times in an afternoon. If you're less than good, you will get to hit it away more often.

Then, out of all this...logic, someone shouts "winter rules" and they get to move the ball to a better location before they hit it. It can be 100 degrees out there and you still get to shout "winter rules." I propose the theory that these people don't know what winter is! Winter rules should be limited to rules that are required to make an activity possible during the season of winter. For example, driving a car should make allowances for "winter rules."

Anybody who navigates around in a car in a Great Lakes winter knows what I mean when I say we are entitled to a break in the rules. Now I know, there are certain precautions we all take and the way we operate our land yachts is greatly different when the roads are slippery. But the rules are still the same! When I say "winter rules" I mean:

Every other stop sign should be covered on bad days allowing you to keep rolling, once you do indeed get rolling.

If you don't like the "lay of your car," you should be

allowed to shout "winter rules" and request that it be moved to a better location before attempting to drive it.

You should be allowed to slide through designated intersections. Perhaps an umpire could be appointed to these intersections to declare you "safe" when you hit the snow bank on the other side.

You should be given the option of having your own snow plow escort, that will proceed you on your way to work, the market, the mall and of course, the boat store.

Should you become stuck in the white stuff, you should have the option of taking a one-mile-per-hour penalty, pulling out a new car and carrying on with your life.

Accidents occurring during inclement weather should not count against your driving record nor your insurance record, unless of course they might qualify for the Guiness record.

OK, enough of the silliness. It's time for the point. In the off season, I occupy some of my spare time by teaching the navigation section of a local boating safety class. I am amazed at the number of people who struggle through sleet and snow, often risking life and limb in order to attend. They'll fly down highways at...highway speeds, knowing that a navigational error of a mere six inches one way or the other could bring them into a close encounter with a light pole or a semi truck.

Yet these are the same people who are "uncomfortable" with the idea of navigating their way along a lake shore because they might stray a half mile off course. They express apprehension at sharing a 1,000-foot river channel with a freighter. And most of all, they express concern at being out there in less than ideal weather.

To all of you who feel this way, or know someone who does, I suggest this: Navigating to a new harbor on the Great Lakes is really no more difficult than finding your way to a new golf course in a different town. In reality, the navigation

John Kenneth Bruce

on the water is a lot more forgiving than the rules of the road on land. All it takes is just a little familiarity, and a desire to find out what awaits you on the other side (of the lake). And that's exactly what I would tell my navigation students tonight, if I weren't stuck in the snow at the end of my own driveway, without a golf cart in sight, anywhere...

Me, My Wife & That Darn Ghost!

Someone recently told me how much they enjoyed our "stupid boat tricks," but then asked me if we didn't have any "stupid winter cruising tricks" too. And actually, we do! And in all fairness, this first one involves me...

It was shortly before Christmas and my wife and I had planned a winter cruising weekend with our fearless (good choice of words) Publishing Editor and his wife. The four of us piled into Jenvey's land yacht and off we went, filled with the spirit of the season, for three days and two nights of Victorian shopping in picturesque Niagara-on-the-Lake, Ontario. The shopping was wonderful and the Falls are beautiful when trimmed in snow, but it was our overnight accommodations that are the center of this tale.

Jenvey had arranged for us to all stay at the infamous, Olde Angel Inn. If you need to be reminded of what this place is infamous for, let's just say that the Angel Inn is reputed to be the most haunted place in Upper Canada. The primary spirit is that of Captain Swayze, a British officer who died here during the War of 1812. Legend has it that as long as the British Union Jack flies visibly over the entrance to the Inn, the ghost stays confined to the main floor and basement. However, should the flag be removed, his spirit is supposed to roam the entire building searching for those (probably Americans) who are responsible.

John Kenneth Bruce

We had a lovely room on the second floor. As you entered, there was the bed and at the far end of the left wall, a door that led to our private bathroom. It was small, but directly on the bathroom's opposite wall was another door that led to our sitting room. Jenvey had gotten us a suite! The sitting room was long and narrow with a small television and a love seat. There was also another half-bath at the far end. The rooms were arranged so that a person lying in bed could look through both bathroom doors and see the TV screen. Next to the bed was a window that overlooked the Inn's Regent Street entrance and just outside our window, flew the famous Union Jack...floodlighted and all. Rest assured, this flag would be flying and visible twenty-four hours a day!

This had all the makings of a most romantic weekend. I blush at confessing to you, but my wife had even bought me a special gift to wear in our room for this weekend and surprised me with it on our first night there. Relax, it was a pair of silk boxer shorts bearing the multiple images of Daffy Duck dressed as Santa Claus. (Thanks, Avon lady!) Obviously a turn-on to my wife, I wore the shorts to bed.

However, some things come back to haunt you...no excuses for the pun. It was our second night there. At around 4 A.M., my wife awoke and decided to use the bathroom. Of course, in the process of crawling out of that four-poster bed, she woke me, too. She flipped the light switch for the bathroom, but nothing happened.

"Ooh," she said with some reservation, "the bulb's burned out!" Then she noticed the air-conditioning/heating unit in the wall wasn't working and a quick glance out the window at the street below told her the rest of the story. "The power's out!"

"But I can see the lights on Queen Street," I mumbled.

"It just seems to be just our street that's out..." she cautiously answered.

Now I was awake. I turned over and could see out the window myself. Our street lights were out. Everyone else's were lit. I also noticed that the floodlight illuminating the Union Jack was dark.

"I have a candle and some matches in my bag," said she.

"Get them," said I.

"They're over in the sitting room...would you go get them?"

The thought of stumbling around in the dark, in Upper Canada's most haunted inn, in my Daffy pants was, shall we say, less than appealing.

"Why me?" I asked.

And, with a great swallow of suffragette pride, she stammered: "Because you're the man!" And after all that talk of equal this for equal that, too!

We eventually agreed to go together. We cautiously stepped into the pitch dark bathroom, me leading the way and my wife, grasping my upper arm, dragging along behind. I could not believe it was so dark. Then I realized that the door to the sitting room was closed...all but about an inch.

"Who closed the door!?" I whispered. I certainly didn't want to surprise anyone that might be on the other side!

"I did," said she. "I didn't want anyone peeking in!"

There was no point in discussing the probability of encountering fifteen-foot-tall peeping toms on the Ontario Peninsula in early winter. I ever-so-cautiously reached out into the darkness and gave the old door a nudge. It slowly swung open as if it were a prop in some 40s thriller, complete with creaking hinge and all. Eventually, it bumped to a stop against the wall in the sitting room. The moonlight through the sitting room windows barely illuminated the outline of the furnishings and shed darn little light into the bathroom itself. It was then I became aware of how tight my wife's grasp on my arm had become.

"Did you do that?" she whispered in panicked tones.

I suddenly realized, in the darkness, she had not seen my other hand shove the door. To her, it appeared to have opened on it's own. I quickly thought of all the nights I had to run to the store because she had forgotten to get milk on her way home. I thought of all the walls I had painted, holes I had drilled, things I had hung, only to redrill, rearrange and repaint. I thought of the wonderful opportunity that had just been handed me and God, I wanted to tell her no.

But I am a coward. I thought about the death grip she had on my arm and about how much I enjoyed having this arm attached to my body. I thought about how she would never speak to me again during the rest of my undoubtedly short life. Then I thought about how she would wake every other guest in the Inn, who would pound-in our door and discover my crumpled remains on the bathroom floor, clad only in my Daffy pants. I turned to her to say yes, and reassure her that it was not some ghostly hand that had opened the door, but somehow, out of my mouth came the words: "No, did you?"

Then things got interesting. She cut off all circulation in my arm. In the subdued light, I could see she was screaming, but no sounds came from her open mouth. She was running away, that is her feet were moving. She was really pickin' 'em up and puttin' 'em down but she was going nowhere...probably because she was still tied to the dock...my arm. I knew there was a pending explosion and in the face of pure terror (her face was pretty scary!), I chickened out.

"Oh, you mean the door? Yeah, I did that!"

I need not tell you the details of the conversation that followed other than it will be a long time before I forget this stupid winter cruising trick. We scrambled for the candle and set it on the shelf in the bathroom. It made a perfect night light, not that anyone in our room was going to get any more sleep that night, but it did take the edge off the darkness. I'll admit that I positioned it so what light there was, did shine out the window at least in the general direction of the Union Jack.

Very oddly, just as the sky was starting to gray-up with the approaching sunrise, the power came back. The bathroom lit up bright (that was a start!) the heat kicked on and the floodlight on the Union Jack went back on vigil. Was it Ontario Hydro solving the problem, or was Swayze just done cruisin' for the night? I don't care. How scary can the ghost be when compared to the wrath of my wife?

Let's All Do the Mast Step...

Not that long ago, I helped Ken Miller drop his mast for the season on *Devil's Dream II*. Do you think that's odd that a devote powerboater would help a rag bagger? Not here at Terry's Marina. It's a kind of do-it-yourself haven for boaters and we're all in it together. It's not uncommon to see powerboaters helping short-handed sailors with yard chores...as you will also see sailors helping to heft outboards, tilt outdrives and fog engines.

So here I was, helping Ken drop his mast at the community gin pole. For those of you not familiar with the process, there's a special cut in the canal for this with a big, hand-operated crane on one side...Well, it's hand-operated now. It used to have a motor but somebody broke it. Now, Terry has put an old steering wheel on it and you crank...forever.

Anyway, this crane literally lifts the mast off the deck. Then, someone carefully guides the bottom end back as you lower it, horizontally, onto the deck of the boat. This past fall, it all went so smoothly. It made me think back and remember last spring when it didn't go so well...and now qualifies as a stupid boat trick!

Last spring, we were doing the opposite: You tie the mast near its center to the gin pole hook with a collar made from a heavy dock line. When you get it high enough, you can swing the mast base down to the mast step, attach the rigging and as far as this powerboater is concerned, you're done! I know, the sailors will then go back to their slips and tighten and tune that rigging for hours. But I'm getting away from the story.

Last spring was Ken's first full season with this newer boat, a Tartan 34 with a keel-stepped mast, i.e. the mast is extra long, and doesn't stand on the deck top, it gets lowered through a hole in the deck and stands on the boat's keel! But let's get to the good stuff:

Last spring, Ken motored *Devil's Dream II* around to the gin pole for the much-awaited mast-raising. We were all there to watch as well as help. Ken left the motor running. He wanted the engine to be nice and warm for the spring oil changing when he got back to his slip.

Painstakingly, he tied a comfortable loop around his mast and secured it to the crane's hook. He wanted to make sure he had extra leeway to handle this huge, delicately balanced mast, that would soon be hoisted so high, up there in the air...above our heads. We all took turns with the steering wheel, which cranked the winch, which raised the mast, above the boat that Ken rebuilt. Ken, struggled to maintain control of the base-end of the heavy stick. It was hard work and us crankers all worked up a good sweat as we spelled each other frequently from this laborious task.

As the hook reached the top of the crane, Ken maneuvered the base of the mast over towards the hole in the deck through which, it would be carefully lowered. But then the unexpected happened. About two inches shy of the mast-step hole, the crane came to a stop...we had run out of cable. The hook was as high as it was going to go, there was no more hoist to be had. Yet we were still two painful inches from victory!

What happened? Two things: First, the water was high that spring, record highs in our end of the lakes as a matter of fact. Since the water was taller, so was the boat, and the gin pole, being on shore, didn't move. There was less room to hoist. This, while an inconvenience, was not a terrible problem. Terry's Marina has a fairly large gin pole, but Ken, in his careful generosity, had tied an overly long hoisting rope around the mast. It could have easily been six or seven inches shorter, and we only needed two!

We all talked about it...casually, as Ken struggled to contain the delicately balanced mast. In fact, we all talked about it at much more length than need be. This was Ken's lesson for being long-roped and short-sighted. We had two options: Lower the mast, shorten the rope and start all over again (and since we were very "cranky" we didn't want to do that) or we could lower the boat in the water!

How? Ken protested the idea of opening the sea cocks and taking on water, but whatever we were going to do, "please hurry!" Our second plan went into action. If you can't take on ballast from below, do it from above. One by one, we climbed on to the deck of the boat. In the way of "people ballast," our portly Publishing Editor climbed on first and took a seat right on the bow pulpit. And then we added more, and more, to the point where all but one of us (Ken's diminutive daughter, Rachel, who would man the crank to lower the mast the first few inches) was standing on the bow of Ken's boat. It worked! It was crowded up there, with about a dozen or so spectators milling around and offering Ken the inevitable advice and opinion. But the boat had sunk low enough to at least get the project done! Then the stupid part happened.

Up the canal comes the County Sheriff's Marine Patrol. On board, a single officer, young, brimming with inexperience and ready for action, One look at Ken's overloaded, listing boat and he was headed right for us with ticket book in hand.

"Good afternoon, sir...Don't you think you have a few too-many people on board to be operating this boat?"

Stupid Boat Tricks

"Operating?" Ken coughed out in amazement, motioning to the array of dock lines.

"Your engine is running, the boat is in operation...Do you have life jackets for all these people?"

When it was all over, Ken held two tickets, one for too many people and another for not enough life jackets. A day late and a dollar short. But lucky for Ken, a judge saw the stupidity behind the rookie's behavior and threw the citations out. However, for the rest of last season, we all spoke of the fine dance Ken held on his deck, how elegant the affair was...but complained about the cost of the tickets.

A Bridge Too Far...

I never realized these little tales of woe would be so popular with you people out there. It seems everybody likes a good tragedy...especially when it's not their own. But this time, we have been asked to change the names to protect the guilty, as well as our own liability. That should tell you right away that this one is exceptionally stupid, yet incredibly true.

In a well-known Great Lakes town, lived a successful, well-known medicine man who was most-respected amongst his fellow, surgical-specialty colleagues. We shall call him Dr. X. Dr. X had it all. Family, big house, fancy cars, booming practice and a reasonable amount of time off to enjoy these things his scalpel earned. There was just one thing missing from Dr. X's life—a boat.

Dr. X had always wanted a boat. A sailboat, specifically. One he could use to cruise and explore these Great Lakes. But family, career and other responsibilities had somehow managed to keep the Good Ship *Snake Oil* hanging on the refrigerator instead of sailing the several lakes. That is, until one fine day.

On that day, the good doctor and his wife looked around to see that the nest was empty! There were no football games to attend, no dance lessons, no choir practices, no conferences or any of the multitude of other things that had kept

Stupid Boat Tricks

them busy for so long. Now it was time. Time to take the Good Ship *Snake Oil* off the refrigerator and put her in a marina.

The dealer was visited and checks were written and it would only be a matter of a few short weeks before commissioning day. Dr. X planned his time well. He'd signed up to take a safe boating course between now and then, but a couple of emergency cranial-ectomies and several gastro-infarction bypasses had prevented him from attending most of the classes. He never finished. His buddy and neighbor, Bob the Plumber, had offered to take him out on the water and show him the ropes and the local hazards. Bob had been boating for years and was willing to share a dock with Dr. X at the local marina. But both times they had scheduled it, Dr. X had to go out of town on the last minute junket. In fact, commissioning day arrived long before Dr. X had imagined.

But commissioning day was glorious! The spring sun shone warmly and gentle breezes filled the air at the dealer's commissioning dock. And there she was, the Good Ship *Snake Oil*, a rather expensive though not terribly large pocket-cruising sloop equipped with all her hand-laid, state-of-the-art electronical finery. The salesman pointed and mumbled incessantly as Dr. X and the Mrs. explored their new pride and joy. All too soon, the engine was started and dock lines were parted. The Good Ship *Snake Oil* was underway. Now, all that stood between them and the open waters of the lake, were a half-mile of river traffic and the Main Street drawbridge.

The trip down the river was not too eventful, save for the occasional passing boat that shouted something about "no wake speeds" but Dr. X just smiled and waved back as the several-ton sailboat chugged along at nearly five knots. The good doctor sat proudly at the tiller, his wife positioned strategically on the bow, holding on to the forestay. Finally, they rounded the bend and they could see it...their home marina and the open horizon of the Great Lake, just on the other side of the Main Street drawbridge. In his excitement, Dr. X tapped the throttle up just a little bit more.

Meanwhile, the bridge tender was startled to see the shiny new sailboat come charging around the bend in the river. He looked at his watch; it was fifteen minutes before the next scheduled opening and with the morning traffic on the road that day, he could make no accommodations. This skipper would just have to tread water for a while.

But closer and closer the sailboat came and it showed no signs of slowing down. The bridge tender watched in wonder as the boat drew closer and closer. Surely the skipper saw his bridge. It must blot out a major piece of the sky from their viewpoint! But by now the sailboat was so close it would have trouble stopping let alone treading water. The bridge tender bolted from his control house and leaned over the rail of the drawbridge, waving his arms frantically.

Meanwhile, on the deck of the Good Ship *Snake Oil*, Dr. X and his wife saw the nice man waving from the bridge and returned his exuberant greeting. The bridge tender sounded five short emergency blasts on his air horn. Dr. X honked back as his wife smiled and waved like the queen of the parade. Finally, the bridge tender ducked for cover.

The forestay hit the bridge first. It bent with a horrible, resonating sound and briefly pulled the mast forward. Then it snapped loose from its deck plate on the bow, narrowly missing Mrs. X as it shot towards the masthead. A several-ton sailboat moving at over five knots creates an incredible amount of inertia. It was far more than any rigging could withstand. The boat continued on under the bridge, the rigging did not. Once the forestay was gone, the shrouds were next to follow, snapping and ripping out deckplates as they gave way.

The mast was raked back and started to fall towards the cockpit. Being the quick and decisive surgeon he is, Dr. X

Stupid Boat Tricks

avoided all injury in exchange for an early season swim in the river. The mast fell on the pedestal steering and somehow, perhaps by act of the Deity, stretched the engine compression cable as it ripped the pedestal from the deck, silencing the iron beast below. Men at the shoreside gas dock threw a line to Mrs. X and secured the Good Ship *Snake Oil* while a passing fishing boat pulled Dr. X out of the river.

As he came aboard he shivered and he sputtered and he swore vengeance on the responsible party.

"What do you mean?" asked one of the fishermen.

"Well, the guy who repairs the bridge!" Dr. X shouted. "This bridge obviously malfunctioned!"

It seems the good doctor, despite his education and social standing, had been living all his life under a grave misconception. He genuinely believed that this drawbridge, like those on the Lionel train set he had as a child, were automatic. He was confident, right up to the moment when the mast hit the concrete, that the bridge would sense his approach and spring open, allowing him to pass much like the doors at the supermarket.

Oddly enough, this did not discourage the doctor. and his wife from pursuing their cruising dreams. The boat was repaired and parked in the marina for the rest of the season while the couple took boating courses, learned about their vessel and obviously, about navigational hazards. Several years have passed since this incident and I am glad to tell you the Good Ship *Snake Oil* has made several passages and inter-lake voyages without incident. It just goes to show you that even the most competent of cruisers can have a very stupid beginning.

Dad Will Never Know...

This particular stupid boat trick illustrates two important principles: First, you should never underestimate the powerful allure of boating, and two, some of the best stupid boat tricks may be old stupid boat tricks! This particular story was told to me by an aging gentleman after a speaking engagement and I hope you enjoy it as much as everyone at my table did that night.

It was the early 1960s along the rural inlets and bays of Green Bay, Wisconsin. Two teenage lads, we shall call them Bill and Bob, were best of friends and next door neighbors along this secluded shore. Among everything else in life, these two boys loved boating. After all, there was a small, shallow bay right there with all kinds of coves and backwaters to explore and plenty of fish for two young men to catch.

But alas, Bill and Bob had no boat of their own and their fathers did not appreciate them taking their fishing boats out on summer afternoons without them. But this summer would be different. The two pals were convinced that if they couldn't take out their fathers' boats, they would build their own!

This would have to be a shoestring operation because not only did they have no boat, but they had no money and in this rural community, no real way to earn any either. But teenagers can be creative. A few miles up the road, a small housing development was taking shape. In the evenings, the two boys would ride their bikes up the road and rummage through the scrap pile looking for any useable, left-over piece of house they might convince into becoming a boat.

Over the course of a couple of weeks, they did indeed secure enough scrap two-by-fours to actually build a frame for a simple boat. She would be about ten-feet long, about four foot on the beam and predominantly flat-bottomed.

Next would come the covering. But there were no scraps in the heap big enough for this job. So they scraped together their life savings and rode their bikes to the lumber yard down the bay. Again, funds were limited and when they were done (read: broke) they had purchased three sheets of quarter-inch exterior plywood. It took them hours to transport the wood home on their bikes, and in retrospect, it would have been easier to carry it the four miles than to try to steady the sail-like package on bicycles. But they did it!

The next several days of their summer vacation were devoted to cutting the wood to fit their ribs, nailing, caulking and painting. Fortunately, the remaining supplies they needed were found in either one father's garage or the other. When she was finished, she was grand! Bright red, low-slung, and plenty of room for the two of them. She looked fast, even standing still.

On that fateful morning of first launch, after fathers had left for work and mothers were engrossed in household chores, the two lads launched their boat from the end of Bill's dock and what joy, she floated...she didn't leak...and the oars they had "borrowed" from Bill's dad worked perfectly.

But after an hour or so of rowing around off the end of the dock in the fast, sleek-looking craft, they began to think thoughts of power...real power!

"Wouldn't it be grand if we had a motor for this thing?"

Stupid Boat Tricks

Bob thought out loud.

"It wouldn't take much to move this boat, she's pretty light," said Bill

"Just a few horses would be all we'd need," dreamed Bob.

"Like that old, ten, two stroke on your dad's boat," added Bill.

The two boys looked at each other. Bob's dad did indeed have an old Mercury outboard on his fishing boat. It was a ten-horsepower, two-stroke powerplant of early fifties vintage and with Bob's dad at work, it wasn't being used right now.

"It's only a test, for our new boat," said Bill.

"Dad will never know," said Bob.

And within minutes, the aging outboard and it's fuel tank had been transferred to the little red boat.

What an improvement! What excitement! The same ten horses that pushed Bill's dad's heavy rowboat along at a "decent clip" turned this lightweight dinghy into a rocket ship! The flat bottom made it perfect for planing and the weight of the two teenagers gave it just enough ballast to go whipping around in hairpin skids and turns. Yes sir! Just scoot across the bay at what seemed like break-neck speed, throw the handle on the motor off to the side and hang on tight as that little red rocket ship side-slipped and then dug in to go shooting off in a different direction.

However, the boys had bought quarter-inch plywood because they could not afford half- or three-quarter-inch. And there's only so much a quarter-inch transom can take...and after several hard turns to the right, the red rocket turned, but the motor and the top six inches of the transom did not. In fact, they parted company. And there they sat, dead in the water with the outboard and the remains of the fuel line sending up bubbles from the bottom. The concept of "dad will never know" was rapidly fading with every bubble that broke the surface.

Fortunately, the water in this end of the bay was shallow. Fortunately, there was enough transom left on the boat that it was still seaworthy. And fortunately they had a hank of rope on board and after some struggling and desperate effort, the two boys managed to pull that old Mercury into the boat and they preceded to row for home.

Meanwhile, back at the dock, out behind the garage, the boys went to work on the outboard. First they replaced the fuel line with a spare hanging in the garage, being sure to rub it in the dirt first to properly age the surface to most closely resemble the line they had broken. Then, they worked on the motor, removing the cover, drying all the water and contacts they could find and finally, blowing all the water out of the carburetor.

With a quick prayer, they primed the engine and would you believe it...it started on the second pull! I don't know if the Mercury folks are reading this or not, but I can tell you that these two teenagers have bought no other brand out of pure thankfulness for the past four decades! They quickly put the engine back on Bob's dad's boat, ran it for a few minutes more, and then made themselves scarce for the rest of the day. They now had full confidence that "dad would never know."

"To this day," my story teller concluded, "those boys have no idea that I know all about it...but my grandsons do!"

"What tipped you off?" I asked Bob Sr.

"That motor hadn't been that clean since the day I bought it! Put that together with a little red paint on the engine cover, a chunk of red plywood buried in the trash and a hunk missing from their transom...and you'd be surprised about how much an old man can figure out..."

"I'll Run Circles Around Ya!"

My father reminded me of this stupid boat trick that happened a very long time ago…and I was there. When I was a kid, my grandparents had a cottage on one of those inland lakes that connect to Lake Michigan through a small river or short channel. You know what I mean, there are dozens of them up both shores of the big lake. I'm just not going to tell you which one.

The advantage to this arrangement is that you have immediate access to the big water, if you want it. But you also have a perfectly protected bay/harbor/lake where you can keep a small dock, a canoe, or even a pontoon boat. It's sort of an inland Great Lake…This is where I spent my summers. This is where I learned about the lakes and boating. My grandparents' cottage was rather like "community property" within the family. We would spend our vacations there, so would my uncle and his family and of course my grandparents were there much of the time.

This entire community of shoreline cottages was built during the 1920s, often by those who were finding their extra money on Wall Street, or in other equally speculative ventures. People like my grandparents sat at home and saved a little here and a little there hoping to someday have their own cottage. When the Great Depression came, all those cottages changed hands. Those who had built them with paper fortunes found they had to sell what was real to those who had been patiently saving, people like my grandparents.

Everyone who bought one of these cottages in the early 30s got a heck of a deal...and they usually paid cash, something the original owners didn't have. The new owners found they had a lot in common and it soon became a very close-knit, vacation community. So close-knit, that over thirty years later, in the mid 1960s, all these cottages were still owned by the very same people...they had all grown old together. I tell you all this because without the relationships, this stupid boat trick wouldn't have happened, or, could have had a tragic ending. It's the people who make the difference.

Anyway, of all the people who had grown old together here, none was older than Bill M. Bill was in his 90s then and had been a widower ever since I could remember. In his advanced years he had become hard of hearing, hard of seeing, and some of the thought process had become hard too. I remember as a young kid walking down the cottage road, being told that if I heard a car, step off to the right shoulder unless it was that big red Oldsmobile! Then we were to step up on to one of the neighbor's porches.

Bill was a character. A nice enough guy but when confronted with his own forgetfulness, his own short comings of advancing age, or his habit of falling asleep at the darndest times, he could become quite cantankerous and difficult to live with. He once fell asleep while smoking and set a fire that did quite a bit of damage to his cottage. He once fell asleep at the supper table, fell off his chair and accidentally killed one of his cats. Bill could be a dangerous man while asleep. But if you dared to challenge him or his skills, he could be downright nasty!

"I can still run circles around you, young fella!" he would often shout at just about anyone.

Stupid Boat Tricks

One hot calm summer day, I was sitting out by the dock with my grandfather, just watching the water and the boats go by when we heard the unmistakable "putter-putter" of Bill's pontoon boat. Bill had built the boat himself from scrap pieces and oil drums many years before. He had a small outboard on the back that managed to somehow push it through the water. But like Bill, it wasn't going to win any ribbons. But at least it ran regular, which is more than could be said of Bill.

We watched as he puttered out towards the small buoy a ways off the end of our dock where he would hang a sharp left before heading for the little cove on the far end of the lake. We watched. Bill turned. But then he kept turning until he was heading back to his cottage.

"Must of forgot something," muttered my grandfather.

But Bill kept right on turning...a full 360 degrees and then around again! It seems he had done the unimaginable. He had fallen asleep in his deck chair right in the middle of a hard left turn! Other neighbors noticed and came down to our dock to inquire since we were sitting there and obviously in charge of the entire lake.

"Is he dead?" one asked.

My grandfather picked up his favorite binoculars.

"Nope, he's snorin'. Probably easier to wake the dead the way he's goin' at it."

"What do we do now?"

"Nothin'" came the surprising answer from my grandfather.

Then they all stood around and scratched their heads and decided he was right. If they woke Bill up, there'd be the devil to pay. He'd be cantankerous for the rest of the summer after being embarrassed so. But right now he was locked into a hard left turn, harmlessly circling a buoy on a quiet weekday afternoon...and we all could keep an eye on him! Eventually he'd wake up, adjust his course and we could all pretend we didn't see him.

Bill's naps were unpredictable. He could sleep like that for a few more minutes...or a couple of hours or so. So we watched. We took turns. Whenever a boat would come puttering down the channel, my grandfather (or whoever was on watch at that moment) would step out to the end of the dock with a boat hook my grandfather had tied a red shop rag to, and get the skipper's attention, then point to Bill. It didn't take more than that. We lived at a secluded, no-wake end of the lake and everybody knew Bill. Everyone quietly motored around him, although he did unwittingly pose for a few photographs!

Eventually the laws of physics came into play as they do in the time-space continuum and with a loud sputter and spat, Bill's outboard ran out of gas. Maybe it was that jerky noise, or perhaps the sudden silence that awoke him, but whatever the cause, Bill awoke with a start at the very same moment my grandfather was at the end of the dock with his boathook and red flag.

Thankfully, my grandfather was a quick thinker. Bill knew that everybody knew he never left the dock without a full tank. How could he run out?

"Drift this way Bill! Must be a heck of a gas leak you sprung!"

Bill's face lit up. He had an out. That's it! Obvious to him, he had been circling the buoy long enough to run out of fuel, but apparently my grandfather hadn't seen him until just the last turn. What luck! Face had been saved and no one knew the truth.

Bill continued to run circles around us all for several more years until he passed away in his sleep, one cold winter night at home.

The Political Season

As a function of my regular employment, I travel a lot. I'm in and out of airports or cruising the freeways of this country's biggest cities far more often than I would like to admit. One of the few advantages of this lifestyle is that it gives me time to observe. And lately I've had more time to observe than usual. That's because I've spent more time waiting than usual. And why would I be waiting? My observations tell me it's because Political Season is now in full swing.

That's right. What with this primary and those caucuses and the endless lines of babies to kiss (interesting euphemism...simply supplant "baby" for "butt") those lovable candidates are traveling even more than me! And somehow we seem to be going to the same places at the same time. I know, because I have spent an unusual amount of time waiting for them to get out of my way.

Imagine, you're in an airport concourse, hopelessly shuffling along when suddenly you grind to a crowded halt. No one knows why, so everyone pushes and shoves as a way of venting frustration. Suddenly there is a burst of activity at the concourse intersection and a squadron of video cameras circles a platoon of not-so-Secret Service agents which encircle the man of the hour. I say "of the hour" because in these politically volatile times, some of these guys' campaigns exist from hour to hour. And as you sit there, caught in the concourse, held in a holding pattern or grid-locked on the entrance ramps as the freeway is closed for the "limo races," an hour is about what you will lose.

I've been putting this time to use, thinking. I think about who it is I'm waiting for and why. I also think about what I would rather be doing if I wasn't stuck here. Now, if you link all those thoughts together, you will come up with one unified question: When was the last time we had a president who was a big-time boater?

FDR was into boating. Specifically, he loved sailing. Eisenhower didn't seem to do any boating after D-Day. I guess, once you've done that, the Chris Craft just loses its appeal. Kennedy did a lot of sailing as a kid but his back injury (which he got while boating) kind of kept him away from it in later years. Reagan didn't boat, except in the movies.

But George Bush was a boater. I remember seeing publicity pictures of him during his first campaign at the wheel of his speedboat. But when he ran for re-election, the pictures and the boat were gone. He didn't win. Maybe there's a message in that. Or maybe it had something to do with that luxury boat tax and all those user fees we're still trying to get rid of. Either way, he rode (instead of sailed) off into the sunset. Note: I refuse to make any white-water-rafting jokes in reference to yet another President.

But where does that leave us for the next election? I have not seen one candidate express any interest in anything nautical. Amusing or not, this should be a warning. I am reminded of a phone conversation Jenvey had with a west coast client last year. This man was amazed to hear that we had lighthouses in the Great Lakes. He couldn't understand why the freighters just couldn't navigate by the lights from the cottages on shore.

All humor aside, this is dangerous thinking. If someone with this misconception were to ever reach high office, what do you think would happen to our Coast Guard funding?

Stupid Boat Tricks

How about the Army Corp of Engineers in this region? ("You can't do that without approval from the Corp of Engineers, and they can't afford to come here, so tough!") How about funding and direction for any project that dredges, dikes, cleans, maintains or enforces anything that protects our Great Lakes?

As long as we are in the process of deciding who's going to run this country for the next several years, perhaps these are questions we, as Great Lakes residents, should ask. I encourage you to attend those town meetings and other "meet the candidate" functions this season. Don't be afraid to raise your hand and ask a Great Lakes pertinent question. Hey, ask him the lighthouse question from above! But ask it backwards. Ask him: "Did you know freighters in the Great Lakes have to navigate by the lights from the cottages on shore?" And if he says, "Well, we'll just have to build those boys some lighthouses," don't vote for this man. If he says, "What happened to the Detroit River Light, Presque Isle and Round Island?" give him your vote.

You may laugh at this but in all seriousness, a number of years ago, a leading candidate for the high office pulled up in front of a UAW hall in Detroit to address a large group of laid-off auto workers who had lost their jobs to outsourcing and foreign competition. His mode of transport? A brand new Mercedes Benz! The UAW boys wouldn't even let him in the door. Yes, they literally turned him away. But the news cameras rolled as the baffled candidate strode back to his car. It seems the man had absolutely no understanding as to why they would treat him like that. Go figure.

In closing, I did call the offices of most of the major candidates and asked if they would be interested in coming to the Great Lakes for a debate on the shores. (Beautiful backdrop, don't you agree?) Sadly, the idea was killed by the Secret Service. They were concerned too many of the candidates would try to walk on it, rather than stand next to it...

The Big Switch

Here's a classic one for you. A perfect example of a little knowledge being a dangerous thing. Unfortunately, this is one of those cases where I'm forced to change the names to protect the guilty...and our liability.

New Guy Navigator was his name. He had bought his first cruising boat for the Great Lakes in the fall of the year and spent the winter months preparing for the coming season. He bought equipment, toys and anything else the new possession needed. But the one thing he couldn't buy in the boat catalog was time. He didn't have enough time to take a basic boating course.

If anyone should have taken the course, it was New Guy Navigator because he was coming into boating cold. That is, he wasn't from a boating family, he had never crewed with buddies before, in fact, his only true boating experience dated back to scout camp and the canoe docks on lake "Betcha-gonna-tip-it" several decades ago. And now, here he was, the proud owner of a twenty-eight-foot cabin cruiser equipped for the adventure from Hell.

"But that's OK!" he said. "I'm an excellent self-teacher! Just give me a good book and I can learn anything!"

And so it was. He sat down with the Chapmans and other such nautical references as his schedule allowed, and he taught himself the important parts of boat handling and

Stupid Boat Tricks

navigation.

I must admit I was honestly impressed by his self-attained skills. I would quiz him from time to time when our paths crossed at social functions or elsewhere in the neighborhood and he always seemed to come up with the right answers. Personally, I teach the public boating class for my local Power Squadron and have my own set of beliefs about new boaters and safety instruction. But New Guy Navigator's skills caused me to doubt my hard-cast notions...that is, until the boats hit the water that spring.

It was early in the season. New Guy Navigator had by now consumed about every book and every article on piloting and coastal navigation. He had the math and the chartwork down pat. He had read personal accounts from other boaters about their experiences in rough weather and periods of limited visibility, like night time!

It was with great confidence that he took off across the waterway to a small, quaint harbor for a day trip to test his skills and his family's mettle for the bounding main. He found the harbor all right and the narrow channel that led into the docks near the waterfront restaurant. They all had a wonderful time. Such a good time, in fact, that they stayed into the evening.

As the sun was starting to set, his wife asked the all important question: "Will we be able to find our way home in the dark?"

"Don't be ridiculous!" said New Guy Navigator. "At night, the buoys light up like Christmas! There's lighthouses and channel markers too! All we have to do is follow the string of lights home. I read all about it!"

She seemed to relax.

But as a beautiful sunset became a pitch-black night, New Guy Navigator started to realize that things were not as advertised. He couldn't see one single buoy along the narrow shallow channel that had led them to these docks.

John Kenneth Bruce

For some reason these buoys were not illuminated.

Between you and me, folks, you have probably figured out by now that poor New Guy Navigator was under the sad delusion that all buoys are illuminated, and that one man's "Christmas" is another man's "dark and stormy night." While you may find his misconception amusing, it's what happened next that ranks this story with the best of the Stupid Boat Tricks.

In frustration that something was wrong with the navigational lighting system, New Guy Navigator picked up the pay phone in the bar and called the United States Coast Guard. He tersely explained the problem and repeatedly asked them that if it wasn't too much trouble, would they please "throw the switch and turn the buoys on" because he had to get home for a big important meeting in the morning. It was an overworked and exasperated Coastie who gave-up trying to make the logical explanations and resorted to the following tactic:

"I'm sorry, sir, but the big switch is broken tonight. I would strongly advise that you stay put at your dock until we can get it fixed, or until the patrol boat shows up and lights the buoys by hand."

"This is a remote harbor, that could take until morning!" protested New Guy Navigator.

"Probably so, sir. If you would like to file a complaint about the buoy service in your area, you can call 1-800-336-BOAT and tell them exactly what you have told me."

The more astute of you out there will recognize that phone number as the BOAT/U.S. safe-boating course hot line. By calling that number from anywhere in the country, you find out about the whens and wheres of a safe-boating course in your local community. The classes are taught by local organizations such as the Power Squadron and the Coast Guard Auxiliary. BOAT/U.S. provides the toll-free number as a public service.

Stupid Boat Tricks

For those of you who recognized the number, my hat's off to you. That means you've probably called it and I hope you've taken the course. If you haven't, I suggest you give them a call. Just don't tell them about the big switch...they've heard that one already.

What's in a Name?

Our last staff gathering was an eye-opener for me. I was talking to Sandra Swanson about her sweatshirt. You see, Sandra and her husband Bob own a goodly-sized powerboat named *Carpe Diem*, which, for you non-Latin reading readers out there, means seize the day. This is not important to me, but the sweatshirt was!

They always have the nicest sweatshirts, T-shirts, hats and I've been told, even coffee mugs on which the name of their boat has been neatly stitched, embroidered, stamped, engraved or what-have-you. Personally, I know boat owners can take the custom ownership thing way too far, but it is nice to at least have something that sets you apart from sports car buffs, the motor-homers, the pilots and other riff-raff. And since Sandra's was so nice, I asked her where she had them made, and that, my friends, was the revelation of the night!

All of Bob and Sandra's *Carpe Diem* fashion accessories came ready-made out of a mail order catalog! This particular company had a whole selection of *Carpe Diem* items and nautical wear, so much so, that it caused Bob and Sandra to give the same name to their boat. That's right, they didn't name the boat and then discover the clothing, they discovered the clothing and then named the boat to match! How devious, how deceitful, how brilliant!

Stupid Boat Tricks

My mind spun with the possibilities. After all I had been through to dig up old James Bond paraphernalia for my own *Moonraker*, here was a system that gave you full access to the best you could buy and not have to pay custom prices.

Across the room, I spied Don Stockton. After spending a portion of last season boatless, Don had just acquired a relatively new vessel that, as of yet, had no name. Here was someone who could genuinely benefit from this ingenious concept and someone who desperately needed my help to do so!

By the next day, I had persuaded Don and his bride to accompany me and mine to that great mecca of selection, the mall. Here, we would surely find dozens of shirts, sweaters, coffee mugs, baseball hats, duffel bags and other necessities, all emblazoned with a suitable name for a 28-foot Carver Riviera. The process began.

Don didn't leap at some of our first suggestions, but here are a few that managed to bring a tear to his eye: Union Bay, Dockers, Nike, BUM Equipment (there were lots of wearable items with this name, but Don didn't want to start off a relationship with a new boat on the wrong foot), Lands' End, Bugle Boy (Don's wife liked that one and for some reason that made Don blush), No Fear, Cheetah, Nirvana (we all liked that one but you couldn't get a shirt without pictures of these grundgy guys on them), Yes Michigan, My Little Pony, Victoria's Secret (Don liked this one but his wife, seeing her name is Patti, did not), Craftsman (we were going through Sears now), Play It Loud, Fruit of the Loom (desperation was setting in), and my personal favorite, When Grandpa Farts, a poem went along with this one.

Don failed to make a final selection that day. His poor craft remains nameless. But rest assured, we will find a name by Memorial Day and I'm sure it will be one Don can wear with pride. And it's just gotta be one with a ready-made wardrobe!

The Fashion Bug

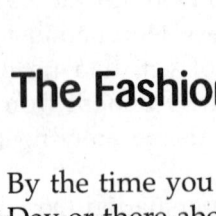

By the time you read this, it'll be Memorial Day or there-abouts, the true official start of summer. I like to get ready early. In fact, my family and I spent most of the past weekend sorting through that box in the basement labeled "summer clothes." This season's efforts have been especially fruitful in that we moved this past year and in the process, uncovered a number of long forgotten boxes labeled "summer clothes." It was sort of a "summer clothes" bonanza.

Now first of all, let's define what the term "summer clothes" really means. These are lightweight articles of clothing geared for the warmer temperatures of the season. Since summer is also a time of recreation, these clothes tend to be casual or even novel in nature. In other words, we're talking about old clothing, devoid of any ability to conceal or flatter the out-of-shape, aging form it attempts to cover and is probably not suitable or appropriate to wear hardly anywhere. And I've got boxes of this stuff!

Not a problem, you might answer. A call to a charity, a trip to the dump, perhaps even a little spontaneous combustion and we could all be at the mall before it closes. But not when your married to Mrs. Frugal!

I didn't intentionally marry Mrs. Frugal. I married the prettiest girl in the dorm, the campus heartthrob. Mrs. Frugal was an apparition that evolved over several years of marriage. Her transformation was gradual but I had recog-

Stupid Boat Tricks

nized all the signs as they appeared: The sale papers hidden under the bed, the coupon clippings, her attraction to blue light...But I can live with Mrs. Frugal. Millions of men do. There is a nationwide support group for wives like this that meets weekly at Target. By herself, Mrs. Frugal is not a problem. But let me tell you about the other woman in my life.

Ms. Boutique is 13 and has now reached the age where she is terribly embarrassed by the mere existence of her parents. Everything in life must be perfect or it shall be a reflection upon our clan for which our descendants will suffer. And of course, reflections are only skin deep and everyone knows that clothes make the man.

Ms. Boutique is manageable in her own right, but put her in the same household with Mrs. Frugal and sparks can fly! They gave up the whole city of Tokyo just so Godzilla and Mothra could duke it out. These two chose me as their battlefield and it was "summer clothes" at dawn.

The first box opened was the most recent in purchase, but I could tell by my daughter's immediate volley of grimaces, it was not the most recent in fashion.

"Eeuuugh!"

I recognized a favorite T-shirt; a brightly colored, grape-infested garment that declared me as a veteran of the Lonz Winery.

"You're not wearing that again this year, are you?"

Questions like that are best answered by professionals. I deferred to Mrs. Frugal.

"Why, it's practically new! Why wouldn't he wear it?"

Although she looked to me, I know questions like this are best answered by professionals. I deferred to Ms. Boutique.

"Mom! It's stupid! Look at it!" She motioned to me for my support in her claim but found only my best, stone-faced look of confusion.

"Now don't say that, your father picked this out himself."

"Well, I'm not going anywhere with you if he wears this!"

John Kenneth Bruce

I filed that away for future reference. My head filled with possibilities when this might be useful. My swim trunks were next to appear.

"Now these have really got to go!"

My daughter held up the multicolored garment comprised of a pattern of strange small shapes all mashed together. Secretly, I was hoping she'd win this one.

"But he's hardly worn it!" I wondered why...

And so the battle progressed. Garments were flying and piles formed on designated areas of the basement floor. T-shirts, Bermuda shorts, a baseball cap with a stuffed fish sticking through it. (Come on! I'm not the only one who bought one of those!) And what the two combatants couldn't immediately agree upon, I had to try on. Now I know how Ken feels.

Eventually they opened a box that contained more of their clothing than mine and as they became lost in the mother-daughter rituals that followed, I slipped away upstairs to the den where my 11-year-old son was busy with the Nintendo machine.

"They gonna let you keep your shirt with the grapes all over it?"

"I don't know, yet."

"How 'bout the hat with the fish stickin' out of it?"

"Nope..."

"Can I have it?"

"...Sure, why not."

And as he toddled off towards the basement to fight for his prize, I became very philosophical. Summer clothes need only be comfortable. The unwritten law of the lakes declares that no matter how strangely you may dress, there will always be someone a little stranger. And if we spend all this time looking at how each other is dressed, we might miss looking at what we've traveled so far to see. And that would be a loss far greater than a hat with a fish sticking through it.

For the Want of a Boom Box...

Late last season at my marina I witnessed the most bizarre exchange of family pleasantries. Well, they weren't actually pleasantries, but they were exchanged by family members and it was indeed bizarre enough to qualify as a stupid boat trick.

I was sitting there in the still-warm September sun, just enjoying the peaceful serenity of the marina and admiring the first boats up on shore for the season. I like to look at boats as they sit in their cradles. It's a side of them you seldom see. But that's not important now. The boat still in the water across the canal from me is the focus of this story.

At first the boat was empty, but then came the people...the family as we will call them; mom, dad and several kids. Out they came to enjoy a late-season, family overnight trip to a nearby port. They were running late and there were concerns about the weather. You can translate that to read they were arguing and bickering before they even set foot on the dock. It went downhill from there.

Soon they were scurrying around in the open cockpit of their sun-chasing I/O, removing tarps, revving engines, stowing luggage and doing a lot of bumping into each other. It was sort of like watching a nautical pinball machine. When one bumped another, there was an equal but opposite reaction as they, in turn, bumped two more "bumpees" who then ricocheted off the outside bumpers and into the corner galley...Maybe it was more like billiards. And all the time, there was a constant flow of chatter from everyone, but I don't think anyone in particular was listening. Maybe they couldn't hear each other over the melodic voice of Alanis Morissette that shouted from the portable boom box...Maybe not. But at least Alanis was making sense.

Suddenly, just as they were starting to back out, there was a loud splash and two or three screams of terror. It was at that moment that everyone, including myself, became painfully aware that the overboard crew member wasn't dad, wasn't mom, wasn't any of the screaming mee mees...it was, unfortunately, the ever popular Miss Morissette whose melodic voice had fallen silent.

Dad scrambled for the boat hook in an overzealous and useless attempt at recovering the wayward boom box. Everyone started calling the child who had dropped poor Alanis overboard, names. And then it started. The blame cycle. Who was at fault for this tragedy? Someone must surely take the fall!

"Thank you for dropping our only boom box in the lake!" Dad sarcastically shouted.

"Well, you bumped me out of the way!"

"I had to drive the boat! What were you doing with the boom box at the rail, anyway?"

"I had to kill a spider!"

"With the boom box?"

"Mom wanted it killed right now!"

"I did not!"

At this point the conversation became confusing and I can only recall certain sound bites, but it went something like this:

"This is your fault, you're gonna pay for it! It's not my fault! That was my CD in there! Thank you for ruining our tunes! Thank you, Mom, for making me kill that poor spider! You've already won me over, head over feet! (Actually,

I think Miss Morissette said this before her fall from grace). You know, if you'd used that spider spray, we wouldn't have this problem! That stuff doesn't work, you ordered the wrong spider spray! That spider shouldn't have been building his web so close to the rail! He's dead! No he's not! You bumped me and I missed him! You know we can't leave the dock with spiders running around here! This is all your fault! It's always my fault! Can't it be yours for just once? Why can't you take responsibility for your stupid actions?"

This was starting to take an ugly turn. I knew that at any moment, lawyers would get involved. There was so much blame floating around, it was getting bigger and heavier by the second and had to eventually land on someone. Caught up in the excitement, I even called my own lawyer to check my liability, after all, I did see it happen. After being told to get a signed statement from three other witnesses and a release from "those without a boom box" I even called Miss Morissette's attorney so he could get his pre-trial disclosures started. Hey, there could have been something in that "head over feet" lyric that was subliminally suggestive. It could happen!

Then, a wave of logic and reason swept over me and I went below to search for propane leaks with a match. Later, I ran into the dad in the restrooms. It seems that without tunes, their boat will not run and they decided to stay the night here in the marina rather than anywhere else on the planet. For the want of a dead spider, a boom box was lost, for the want of a boom box, a weekend was lost...you get the idea. He rhetorically asked me what can you do when something like that happens. What I told him will differ from what I will tell you.

I'll tell you that explosions like these need family therapy. Contrary to popular belief, boating isn't good therapy. You need to have it together in the first place to really enjoy boating, otherwise it will only get worse. I'll also tell you that out on the water, even if only two feet from your own dock, things happen. It doesn't have to be someone's fault. And even if it is, it isn't necessary to prosecute, persecute and convict in front of a jury. Jenvey said it best: If your boating causes you to yell, scream, shout, threaten, call lawyers and endanger those around you, you're not doing it right. So what did I tell the dad? I told him to buy an in-dash stereo and a fly swatter...

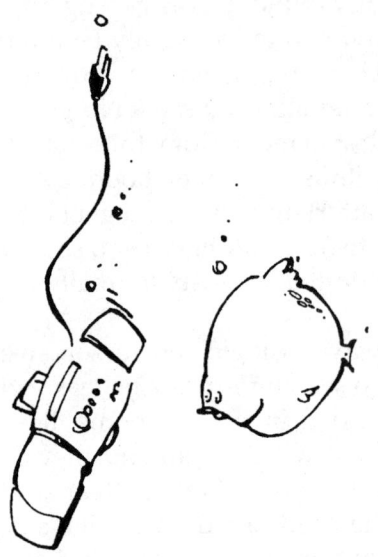

Dick and Jane at the Boat Show

"Look, Jane, Look, Look, Look!" shouted Dick as he poured through the entertainment section of the local metropolitan newspaper. "The Boat Show opens today!"

"Boat Show!" exclaimed his wife, Jane.

"Boat Show!" cried Baby Sally.

So off they went to the Monstrous Memorial Metrodome in the frozen suburb of the metropolis. Dick, Jane, Sally and her teddy bear, Douglas McCleod. The Boat Show was in town!

"Look at all the boats!" said Jane.

"Big Boats! Little Boats! Everybody's Boat!" said Dick.

"But which one is our boat?" asked Baby Sally as she clung tighter to Douglas McCleod.

"I don't know." said Dick. "We will just have to look high and low, low and high until we find it."

"But how do you even buy a boat?" asked Jane.

"See that boat there?" asked Dick.

Jane nodded.

"Do you want to buy it?" asked Dick.

"Oh no!" said Jane. "That boat is too small! There would be no room for Baby Sally or Douglas McCleod."

"Old Captain Smith told me never to buy the first boat you see," said Dick. "Now we have seen the too small boat. Now everything else is fair game!"

John Kenneth Bruce

"Wheee!" cried Baby Sally. "We'll get a big boat! Big enough for me and Douglas McCleod!"

"Big enough for all of us!" squealed Jane.

"As big as we can get!" squealed Dick.

And off they went, into the Boat Show, past the booths with the funny clothes, past the pretty ladies in the tight dresses, past the big ladies in the little swimsuits, and even past the stand that sells Peruvian corn dogs, on a stick.

I can't bear to tell you what happened next. But speaking of the Boat Show, doesn't that sound like fun right about now? Especially the part about the Peruvian corn dogs, on a stick. I really guess my whole point here is that the boat show is a whole lot of fun for everyone, regardless of your boating expertise, regardless of your intent to buy and certainly regardless of your ability to pay. Come on! It's deepest darkest winter out there and these are the only people in town selling swim suits...well, at least wearing them too! But if you should see these three lost souls and the teddy bear at your boat show, follow them. There's apt to be a heck of a deal in their wake!

Politically Correct Cruising

I have just finished my first cruise of the year. It was a simple little overnight, weekend jaunt to a close-by port that wasn't really ready yet for the season. I was their first transient. I pride myself on being the first one to do this or that in any given year. What I had not planned on was being the first to offend the hired help.

As I approached the docks, there was no response from the harbormaster's office on the VHF. Probably not out of the mothballs yet, I thought. But as I drew closer to the empty finger docks, I could see a red-shirted service-personnel-type person seated in the little dock office reading the newspaper.

"Hey, Dockboy!" I called out gaily, confident that I was the first this season to echo my voice around the harbor so.

And sure enough, the red-shirted service-personnel-type person heard my calls, put down the newspaper and stepped out to the pylons to catch my lines.

However, this was no dock boy. This was a very attractive young woman who quickly and professionally helped me secure *Moonraker* to the pier. And then, before leaving, she looked at me coolly and simply said:

"By the way, it's dock girl...."

Unwittingly, I had offended. Well, there was another first for this season. But being the sensitive, caring individual that I am, I decided then and there to make it the last time this season that I offended out of thoughtlessness. (If I'm going to offend, I prefer to do it deliberately and with plenty of premeditation.)

I put some time into this and came up with a set of new names that will be sure to offend no one. Yes, these are the words of Politically Correct Cruising:

The term dock boy is no longer a proper descriptor, unless you can see through your VHF radio and know whether the harbormaster is going to send down a dock boy or a dock girl. dock person seems a little too predictable. I thought of children of the dock, or dock child, but then I remembered being served last season by some who were senior citizens. Dock attendant sounded too much like an airline stewardess...or steward...I guess they had the same problem.

The term dockers seemed to have some merit until it was pointed out to me that the big bad blue jean company might object and besides, grammatically speaking, I am the docker, they are the dockees...and that sounds hopelessly stupid over a VHF. We tried it. With the options being eliminated fast, I was greatly relieved when we hit paydirt. Dock slinger! Why not? It implies ageless, sexless, expertise with a dock and denotes a flavor of the Old West. And everybody loves a cowboy, cowgirl, cowchild, cow attendant...oh hell.

The gas dock is another misnomer that needs correcting. While many of us do indeed buy gasoline at the gas dock, it has been pointed out to me that many of our cruising friends buy diesel fuel there too. Fuel dock seemed a far better term until my young son remembered that the gas dock near our marina is also his favorite place for ice cream and potato chips. In fact, our gas dock is really more like a party store, but party dock just didn't sound right. So we settled on convenience dock. It's clean, descriptive and even new boaters should quickly grasp the concept.

Sea gull is yet another misleading term. While these may be the same birds one finds near the ocean, these are the Great Lakes. But a Great Lakes gull is a mouthful. And calling them just gulls, dredges up too many memories of too many nautical restaurants that label their restrooms for "buoys and gulls."

My daughter came up with the concept of naming them for your own respective Great Lake. We would have Huron gulls, Ontario gulls, Superior gulls and so on. It was Jack Edwards who pointed out that in areas where two or more lakes came together (i.e. the Straits or the Welland Canal), that the birds might fly from one lake to the other and thereby be mis-identified. But the beauty of my daughter's system is that you call 'em as you see 'em, naming them for the body of water you are in right now. This might make it the first bird in history to be able to change its species simply by changing real estate. Awesome!

There are other terms we saw that need to be changed and several we have handled, but we felt these three were enough for you to deal with in one sitting. Perhaps after you have become accustomed to these new vocabulary entries, we will run some more. In the meantime, may you not confuse your knots with your knots, may your out-drives remain in your boats and may your craft always be wave-worthy.

Christmas, Most of All

'Tis the Season to draw near
The family, and spread good cheer,
To celebrate another year
Of love between us all.

The house is decked with mistletoe
And packages, all tied with bows,
Warmed by scented candles glow,
Casting shadows on the wall.

A tree like none I've ever seen,
With tinsel trim and everything,
Lights the room and sets the scene
For guests about to call.

The bitter cold and winter winds
Are beyond the door, where friends come in
Bearing gifts and sheepish grins,
Spilling laughter down the hall.

This season's joy is everywhere,
You can feel the magic in the air,
And see it sparkle here and there,

Stupid Boat Tricks

In the hearts of one and all.

Just watching eyes grow big and bright
As tales of elves in pale moonlight
Bring the squeals of pure delight
From children, big and small.

But sadly, it occurs to me,
There are smiles that will absent be,
Old friends and lovers my heart still sees,
And good times I recall.

So to those I'll miss this time around,
Where ever you are, with whomever you've found,
Know I think of you when I hear the sounds
Of Christmas, most of all…

Boating by the Seat of Your Pants

I've been waiting a long time to get permission to tell you about this stupid boat trick! I could have changed the names to protect the guilty as I have done before, but this one is so much funnier with the correct names in place...especially since the name in question is that of our publishing editor, Bruce Jenvey. Yes, the same lovable guy who glued his trailer to the bottom of his boat and nearly had his hair parted by one of his own flares. (OK, so I'm the one who fired it, but it was his flare!) He has agreed to let me tell you about his famous pants trick.

It was March. Bruce and his father-in-law George Goodling kept their boats in the same marina. It had become standard procedure that Bruce and George would travel out to the marina together in the early season to prepare their crafts for the invasion of the families and the coming barbecues. But here, in the preseason, it was "guy time." They would bundle-up in heavy jeans, sweatshirts and stocking caps, trek out to the marina and work on their respective boats for a while. Then they would find a late afternoon burger and brew at one of the waterfront pubs. These were good times. But there was one brisk March afternoon that has long lived in their memories...and you're about to hear of it.

Back then, Bruce's boat was *Caxambas*—a Seminole

Stupid Boat Tricks

Indian word meaning a hole in the ground in which you pour water—the very same twenty-four-foot, pop-top pocket cruiser that he had previously glued to his trailer. Even though Bruce would never tow this thing again, in the winter the marina still used this now famous trailer as his cradle.

It was convenient. Not too high off the ground. Just a short climb from frame to fender and then swing your leg over the cockpit combing and you were in! Getting down was even easier. Most of the time Bruce just sat on the combing and shoved off, landing on his feet. Given his portliness, it was almost...macho.

But sometimes the best-intended plans of man don't work out. On the particular March afternoon in question, Bruce had been working below while George had finished enough projects on his own boat that he felt comfortable in cutting away his shrink-wrap for the season. That done, he suddenly realized he was tired and very hungry. It was time to hit the pub!

He walked across the boat yard to *Caxambas* shouting words of encouragement to "Wrap it up, let's go eat!" Bruce had been so involved in his own project he hadn't realized how hungry he'd gotten (and that can be pretty hungry!) Food sounded good so he quickly put down the tools, locked up the boat and prepared for a hasty dismount from the cockpit combing...as usual.

But this exit was anything but usual. We are still not certain of exactly what happened that day. There was no video replay, no black box, and George was the only eyewitness. But however it happened, it happened. As Bruce sat on the combing and launched himself over the side, the very crotch of his jeans became hooked on the jib cleat. Fortunately, nothing vital became ensnared, just the aging seams of a pair of Mr. Levi's best.

There was a short ripping noise as the cleat took hold

and Bruce's expected plunge of three feet became one of only three inches. He dangled there in space, upright, too far over the edge to come back and still a foot or two off the ground. George, not yet realizing that anything was wrong, wondered what Bruce was waiting for. He seemed ready to jump...but why all the waving? He stepped closer.

Even the toughest jeans with the finest seams can take only so much and after a few moments of suspense, the inevitable began to play itself out. First it was an inch, then another, but after only a couple of false starts, the stitches in Jenvey's rear surrendered en masse and our portly publisher fell from grace...or is that, without grace? Anyway, it was nearly on Grace, had she been around and George, in her stead, barely missed playing catcher. But there Bruce lay at his feet, the seat of his jeans ripped out from the crotch to the belt loops. A small, errant piece of fabric still clung to the jib cleat.

It took him only an instant to understand the reason for Bruce's slow dismount. But without missing a beat, George took the opportunity to remind him of past tragedies.

"You know, given your track record, I'd thought you'd glued your butt to the side of the boat."

With all snickers and jabs aside, the two still did face one important obstacle: They were hungry, the Green Street Tavern was calling and Bruce only had one pair of pants with him. What to do? After a few minutes of considering their options, a course of action was decided. Bruce cut a large piece from George's discarded, blue shrinkwrap, went to the men's room and quickly fashioned an interior patch for under the seat of his jeans. In essence he was now wearing a large, blue plastic diaper under his jeans and with his sweat shirt tied around his waist, the gaping rip was virtually unnoticeable. They would go to the pub as planned!

But boat yards are wide open places where the wind can whistle against your face...and ears. And Irish pubs are

Stupid Boat Tricks

indoors and can be considered relatively quiet. From the moment they entered the front door, the noise made by rustling shrinkwrap became most evident! It was heard by everyone, though no one was quite certain where it was coming from. Throughout the entire meal, every time Bruce shifted in his chair, there was a flurry of rustling noises. Heads would tilt and people would pause to hear that unusual sound. Of course, the diner leading the crowd, the one who would pause first, tilt his head the farthest, and even cup his hand to his ear...was George Goodling.

I Think She's Trying to Kill Me...

By the time you read this, it'll be March, and if the weather breaks, it'll also be time to start cleaning out the boat. I know, you can't necessarily trash the tarp yet, but I often begin the major process of cleaning out the cabin about now. I start with the galley and at this time of year, I really don't mind this job. Why? Because I know without a doubt, that anything edible I find here, isn't edible anymore. It's the one time of the whole year that I can be certain of what's good, healthy and nutritious...and what could kill you. Sounds like there's a story behind this, doesn't it...

As I have told you before, my culinary skills are lacking. I haven't spent much time in the kitchen ever since that incident with the EPA. But out on the boat, I do try so hard to contribute to this aspect of life. However, and oddly enough, my wife does not seem to appreciate my efforts and quite frankly, I think she's trying to kill me.

Case in point, she and the two young ones take off from the marina for the better part of a day leaving me to relax with a good book.

"Have fun!" she says. "There's plenty to eat here, we'll be back in time for supper!"

Gilligan (the family dog) and I turn on the ball game and stretch out. Around mid-afternoon, we share a ham sandwich. I had no trouble finding the meat in the cooler along with the bread, the mayo and the other amenities to a fine, rainy-day lunch. When she returns, she almost looks surprised to see me up, walking around in the cabin.

"Did you have lunch?"

"Of course!"

"What did you have?"

"A ham sandwich and some—"

"Ham!? You didn't eat that ham did you?"

"Well, yeah..."

"Oh my God! That stuff was a old as the hills! I was going to throw that out!"

"But you said there was plenty of—"

"But not that! Your nose should have told you not to touch that! Do you feel OK?"

"No..."

Now I'm dying. It seemed to me that if it was in with the rest of our food, that it too must be healthy, nourishing and at least edible. Not a trap, a poisonous piece of bait left lurking for the fatally unaware diner. I didn't have the heart to tell her I'd shared it with the dog.

This has happened many times before. Another case in point: Just not that long ago, I started grilling the hamburgers while she was up taking a shower. When she got back, we served up a lovely meal with some beans, cottage cheese and all the other fixings. She even told me how good everything was. I felt so proud. And then I told her it was lucky that we had enough hamburger on board to do this again yet another evening this week. She stopped chewing and went pale.

"Which hamburger did you use?"

"The hamburger in the cooler."

"The old package or the new package?"

I quietly thought it over. Hey, one wasn't wrapped in art deco paper with pictures of Roosevelt on it. Old package? There were two packages, a left and a right. I cooked one.

But my silence spoke volumes and she raced to the cooler. She lifted the lid, looked inside and screamed.

"Oh my God! That stuff was a old as the hills! I was going to throw that out!"

Now she's really bent because both she and the children have been exposed to rancid death, too. I don't understand this. If it's gone bad, if it's too unhealthy to eat, why is it in the cooler with the good stuff? If she was going to throw it out, why didn't she? How did it get to stay there that long that it became a threat to organic life? Why can't I tell the difference between the two?

It's not fair. When I'm working on the boat, I don't leave coffee mugs full of old engine oil on the galley. I don't filter the gasoline through paper cups and put them back in the dispenser. I don't even unclog the bilge with pieces of silverware and then put them away without a good washing first.

You know, I think this all started with the toilet seat. Women world-wide have this passion for wanting the toilet seat left down. Why? Because otherwise, they might fall in. Don't they look first? No, they just want to dash in, expose their nude backsides and plop down on the great unknown. At home I tried suggesting to her that she should look first. After all, perhaps a snake or a rat had crawled up out of the sewer system. But no dice. I did, however, win this battle on the boat. One Saturday morning I climbed back into the bunk and told the harrowing story of how I had just killed a big, ugly, hairy spider as he crawled out from under the edge of the toilet rim. Now she looks first, at least on the boat, and thanks me for leaving the seat up so that she can take a peek without any sudden surprises. But it was about that time, that the food started tasting funny...

Is There Sound in a Vacuum?

Sound does not exist in a vacuum. How could it? There is no air through which sound waves travel. There can be no sound. Well, in breaking news, I now have evidence to the contrary!

Last Sunday, I was at my marina just working on *Moonraker*. No family outing this weekend as scheduled maintenance was due. I was only out during the days and I was alone, busily working on this project and that. I was down in the engine compartment and in no physical position to stand up and converse when my dockmate came along.

"Do you know how to work the new pumpout controller?" he asked.

A word of explanation is in order here. At Terry's Marina, many basic services are free, but they are on a do-it-yourself basis. Head pumpouts also fall in that category. At the end of one canal, a short, stubby white tank with a long hose sits on the sea wall. Through the switching of a pump and valve system, a vacuum is created in the stubby white tank and the contents of your holding tank are sucked inside. Once there, a valve is switched and the pump is reversed so that pressure can build up in the tank to dispel the waste out of the stubby white tank and directly into the township sewer system. Nifty, huh?

Well, we've had the system for a few years now and it used to be that you had to physically turn a key to switch the pump from "pumpout" to "discharge." But that all changed this spring when Terry installed a new, much more powerful, fully automated, security-card key-operated, control head on the same stubby white tank. We knew this because it says so right on the side! It's fully automated. It will discharge and recycle itself when needed. Just swipe it with your key card and pump!

So when my dock mate asked me if I knew how to use this new technological wonder, I was wondering if there was a trick question involved.

"Yes, Roger, I do..."

"Well," he said quite confidentially, "my sons usually do this. Could you help me?"

While the thought of pumping out the contents of Roger's holding tank was most tempting, I restrained myself.

"I'm up to my elbows here, really...it's pretty simple though. The instructions are right on the side!"

"Oh, OK...It really is automatic then..."

"Yup. Just swipe your card through the little slot!" And

Stupid Boat Tricks

then he was gone. But a few moments later he was back.

"There's no valve on this thing, just a pressure gauge. You're sure it's automatic."

"Very Sure." And again he was gone. But then again, he came back.

"What's it mean when the pressure valve says sixty?"

This got my attention. The center of this pressure gauge reads zero, then there is a positive and negative scale on either side telling you whether the pump is sucking (negative pressure in the tank) or discharging (positive pressure in the tank). What bothered me so was the fact that the pressure had reached either sixty. It usually runs at five or ten! There was no danger that the tank was going to implode or explode, there is a safety feature for that contingency. But I know that it will reach a point where it shuts itself down. And then it takes hours to get it to purge and reset itself, and I was planning to use it yet today!

"Negative or positive sixty?" I quickly asked.

"Negative, does that mean it's discharging?"

"No," I drew a half a sigh of relief. At least he hadn't plugged it up. "It means it's ready to go...really ready to go! The valve on the end of the pumpout hose must be closed and it's built up a hell of a suction in there. You'd better let some of that pressure off before it shuts down the system."

"Oh! OK!" And once again, he was gone. This time he didn't come back. Instead, there were a few seconds of peaceful silence during which I accomplished much. But that was all shattered by the pained screams of a woman suffering some heinous torture.

Everyone in the marina that afternoon heard it and came rushing to offer assistance. But when we all arrived at the pumpout, the apparent site of the damsel in distress, we were all repelled by something more heinous than the woman's screams: the great odor that rose in a cloud from Roger's boat.

Let me explain something here. Roger doesn't have a conventional marine head and holding tank. He has a portable toilet conversion. That is, it is a regular chemical toilet with about a five-gallon capacity. To convert it to "permanently installed" status, you cut a hole in the bottom and install a sump kit which attaches to a sanitation hose that terminates in a deck-top pumpout fitting. There is also a vent hose you have to install, but Roger, being eager, lazy and not wishing to drill any "unnecessary" holes in his beloved craft, threw that part away.

Apparently his sons overcame this oversight by slightly opening the flush valve in the toilet before applying the ten pounds of vacuum pressure. After all, air has to get in there to replace the volume of the contents being sucked out. Right?

Roger didn't know this. And in his eagerness, Roger didn't release any of the sixty-plus pounds of vacuum pressure either. He just put the hose over the fitting and opened the valve on the pumpout hose.

His lovely wife (well, she used to be lovely) was below at the time, watching the process from the doorway to the head. We have her eyewitness report from which to reconstruct the tragedy. It seems that the sixty-plus pounds of pressure hit the sealed up port-a-toilet like a sledge hammer.

"Hey, it's a toilet!" I remembered Roger saying. "I bought the cheapest one I could find and put the extra hundred bucks into this great stereo!"

The toilet crunched like an empty beer can, paused a moment and then completely imploded rupturing all it's seams with a great force. But not even sixty-plus pounds of pressure can empty a five gallon potty tank instantly, although it did an amazingly fine job. Those contents that remained in the tank met with the great force mentioned above. And then they decorated everything and everyone in line-of-sight range. Hence the heinous screams which we did indeed hear in what must have been a near perfect vacuum.

While the world of science may doubt our findings and be hesitant to change their written opinions, I was there when the you-know-what hit the fan. I heard the screams. And I was there (but not for long) when Mary Ellen crawled out of the cabin. It wasn't pretty.

Parts Is Parts...

In all modesty and in all humility, I consider myself to be a funny guy. I'm always the one with the quick come-back, the witty phrase and the unexpected pun. I'm the guy that makes people laugh at parties, the guy who can draw smiles from innocent passersby and the guy who gets people to snort liquids out of their noses. I am never at a loss for words, except once. I can think of one occasion when I was speechless, surprised, stunned and blind-sided by a very clever young man working where you'd least expect to find him. Let me tell you about him.

We were on a family cruise along the Wisconsin shore. We lived in Chicago then, and the boat was the predecessor to our current *Moonraker*...OK, we (I) named it *Thunderball*. But that's another story. Anyway, we were planning to spend a few days not that far north of Chicago when unexpectedly the rest of the family called and decided to drive up and meet us for an afternoon!

Suddenly my wife was thrown into the complications of planning a hot picnic meal for six extra people who happened to be in-laws. It's best not to talk to a woman at times like these, especially since I was the one who offered the invite. No, it's generally best to stay out of the way as much as possible and do any chore that is requested of you. And that's where she got vengeance.

Stupid Boat Tricks

"Honey…someone's got to go to the store…"

The store. She meant the grocery store. I hate the grocery store and she knows it! I've been known to perform many household chores without complaint. I've cleaned, I've cooked, I've done laundry. But of all the chores a husband can do, at the absolute bottom of the list for me is the trip to the grocery store. I think it's because with all the aisles and carts, it reminds me too much of the rush-hour commute. (If you think people drive brain-dead on the freeway, check out a grocery store!) Perhaps it's my fear that I'll succumb to cart rage and start throwing produce around, or my hope that someone else will. Whatever the reason, I really hate going to the grocery store.

But she was busy putting the rest of the meal together, corralling the young'uns and cleaning the boat for guests (even though the picnic would be in the park). They were my relatives that were coming. I swallowed hard, smiled meekly and agreed to go.

At least this was a smaller town and I wouldn't be entering some urban mega-liner. This would just be your average American grocery store. Armed with my list, I proceeded on the basic search and rescue mission; finding the right-size box of this and discovering where they hide everything else.

Finally, at the bottom of the list, I came to the meat. I needed to go to the meat counter and have someone wait on me, for a change…and then, I was out of there! I began to feel assured, confident, the usual "me" was returning as the light at the end of the tunnel grew brighter. I strode up to the counter and took a number. I really didn't need a number, there was only one customer in front of me, but I didn't want to take any chances that some pushy, late-coming local, might squeeze in ahead of me and delay my escape from the grocery store. Within moments it was my turn and the bright-eyed, enthusiastic young man began to fill my order. A pound of this, two pounds of that…

John Kenneth Bruce

"You're really stocking up, sir!" he said.

"Well, it's a big family picnic down at the marina and my wife likes to put out a nice spread," I answered.

But there at the bottom of the list was the order I didn't truly understand: chicken parts. How do you order chicken parts? What parts do you get? Fortunately, I didn't have to ask as there was a whole bin under the glass labeled chicken parts, and yes, they were on sale too! My confidence soared. My last stumbling block had been answered in advance and I ordered boldly with a dash of panache.

"...And, some chicken parts, please!"

The young man began to vigorously and rhythmically stack chicken parts on the meat scale.

"How many chicken parts do you want?" he asked.

An evil glimmer came to my eyes. Temptation was too much and I gave in to my own sense of humor.

"Oh...enough to build my own chicken..."

Without missing a beat, without hesitation, the young man reversed the process and starting taking parts off the scale, only to replace them with other parts.

"Well then," he said, "you'll want both left and right legs, otherwise your chicken will run funny!"

He got me! I was without a comeback, without words, completely surprised and now completely off track. I laughed, but not as hard as I did later when retelling this story, and then, not as hard as I have in the years since. I hope that young man got out from behind the meat counter and found some place to put that sense of humor to use.

The Pompeii Pumpout

Right around 1970 I remember Vic Yurick, my high school history teacher, telling me that history is doomed to repeat itself. No, I argued, we were an intelligent species, and once we learned the lesson that history can repeat itself, we can break the cycle! No, he said, that's why it does repeat itself. At the time, I didn't know if it was the pessimism of the late Vietnam war I was hearing or someone far wiser in his years than I...and then I took up boating.

Ralph and his wife Marge bought a smaller cabin cruiser after the nest was empty. It was their perfect weekend getaway and a reasonably well-equipped pocket cruiser, except for one thing: it had a holding tank the size of a bucket. This was unusual, because it did have a full-fledged marine head, not a converted port-a-potty on board. For those of you who may be unfamiliar with the difference, a port-a-potty depends on gravity to transport the contents of the bowl to the tank or storage device whereas a true marine head has a pump. Most often this is a hand-operated pump with a lever. Flip the lever one way and you pump in water from the lake. Flip it the other way and you forcibly pump the water and "what we no longer want" into a waiting holding tank. Ralph's new boat had a marine head all right, but the smallest holding tank I have ever seen.

I think the manufacturers do this to make more room in

the cabin so they can sell the boat on spaciousness. Most buyers don't have to answer nature's call at the moment they are signing the financing papers, and therefore they tend not to think about holding tank capacity—they're thinking about cabin space.

Fortunately for the consumer, there are remedies to this situation. A couple of companies have developed additional holding tank bags you can add to your holding tank system. These bags are tough, durable, and the great thing is they are flexible! You can fit one of these around a corner, into a space where a conventional, hard-sided tank would never go once the boat has been assembled. So joy, you can now utilize wasted space under this cabinet, or that settee by stuffing it full of a large bag of...holding tank juice. Ralph selected the unused storage space under his V-berth.

Why not? It was easy to get to. Just lift up the plywood boards under the cushions and there was all the room under there to work. Just run a hose to the other holding tank and voilà...

All worked well at first, until that fateful morning after the big marina party. Ralph had partied hearty and was now doing gastrointestinal penance for the crimes of the night before. Marge was worse for wear, but sleeping the sleep of the undead in the V-berth while Ralph worshipped the porcelain marine head...Without going into descriptive detail, let's leave it at there was considerable pumping and flushing, intaking and draining, rinsing and even more pumping that was going on that morning.

Slightly stirred by all this commotion, Marge lay there, half awake, enjoying the most unusual dreams. First, she was in an elevator, then ascending into Heaven, then trapped in her car on a mechanic's hoist. It was this panic that completely awakened her to realize that the ceiling of the V-berth was significantly closer than she remembered—and every time her husband pumped, it grew a fraction closer!

Stupid Boat Tricks

A screamed summoned her husband who quickly diagnosed the problem: This expandable bladder tank had now become overfilled, at least for the space Ralph had allotted for its use. It had swollen above the storage area, lifting the boards and the bedding with it. And there was Marge, perched high atop this giant bag of...holding tank juice. She tried to move, but in the now cramped quarters, every shift of her weight threatened to pinch the bladder between the boards and the fiberglass frame. No, it would be best to stay where she was while Ralph moved the boat to the pumpout and relieved the pressure from the outside.

But this would take help. One man alone cannot save his wife from being trapped by a giant bag of...holding tank juice. So soon the boat was tied up in the slip at the do-it-yourself pumpout machine and even sooner there was a small crowd of those of the male persuasion, each ready to do his part to save Marge from her predicament, and each in about as good a shape as Ralph after the party last night. They all huddled around Ralph as he struggled with the deck plate key that would remove the little metal circle that would allow the guy with the hose to signal the guy at the switch so the guy could turn the T-valve...you get the idea.

Now, I mentioned at the top of this story that history repeats itself. Since then you've probably been thinking, "What repeat? Who in the world has ever been in this situation before?" After all, this is space-age technology creating an ultra-modern stupid boat trick. But that's not the history I was referring to. Many years ago, in a city called Pompeii, the townspeople ignored every sign that their nearby volcano was about to go postal on them. And then, suddenly, it did. Many people were instantly covered and forever preserved in a thick coat of volcanic ash. As I recall, it happened early in the morning after a big festival of celebration the night before.

It was at about this same time in the morning that Ralph

finally loosened the deck plate. Inside the cabin, Marge immediately felt a great sense of relief. The giant sack of...holding tank juice suddenly lost tension and quickly returned her bed to is normal position. As she crawled out of the bunk, he gave it a good extra bounce or so to make certain all was flat. Then she crawled out of the cabin and into the daylight.

And there were the men, standing at the hull completely motionless, as if frozen in time, now covered with a thick and dripping coat of...holding tank juice. One witness watching from a nearby flybridge described it best:

As Ralph removed the deck plate, all the men huddled closer in anticipation of doing their part to rescue Marge, not anticipating that the weight of the woman was equal to the mass of the negative pressure conversely and inversely proportional to the force of gravity. Put simply, that giant bag of...holding tank juice worked like a big bagpipe as it played its contents right out of the side of the boat in a stream about three feet long. Of course all the men were within one foot or less from the opening and history repeated itself all over them, all over the ground and followed them to the showers...

Picture This...

The best thing about being the parent of a teenager is you've been there, done that. When they try to pull something and they think they are the first ones in history to dream up this little antic, little do they realize that you got away with the same thing when you were their age...and now you can be there waiting for them when they least expect it.

The worst thing about being a parent is trying to figure out which little stunt they're trying to pull off behind your back this time so that you can figure out which paths to block. If you're lucky, like me, sometimes they'll even help you if you're just patient enough.

As my daughter went through the mid-teenage years, I often felt she was up to something, that she almost always had an alternative motive, or maybe it was just my inability to decipher the female mystique. But I knew she was up to something far more often than she got caught.

As an example, one night at home about a year ago she was treating me so nice. It took me a while to figure out that she wanted to borrow my van for an evening out with her friends that coming weekend. She was shining up to me pretty good, in fact, she was even showing an admiring interest in my other favorite hobby, model railroading. She even went so far as to dust off my old 35 millimeter SLR camera she had confiscated quite some time ago, and polished off a roll of film that had been in there God knows how long. Yes, there were snaps and flashes of wonderful dad at his workbench, tuning up a favorite locomotive and smiling close-ups of me with my prize scenery scapes. And when the film was gone, she feigned poverty and asked me to develop the roll.

Well, it was pictures of me and my trains, so I agreed and the next day I took them to the drug store. Being a little impatient, I even had them develop the film in an hour rather than waiting the two days. But it was when I got my pictures back that I got the real surprise!

As I leafed through the stack, there they were, the shots of me next to the miniature hotel I had built, me holding my prized brass steam engine, me air-brushing a new caboose, my under-age daughter drinking a bottle of beer…A bottle of beer!?

Yes…It seems these shots had been in the camera a long time. So long in fact, that she had completely forgotten what was on them! I continued to go through the stack and filled in most of the blanks for myself.

I recognized the cabin of my boat. I recognized several of her friends…and several of the boys I did not recognize at all. But there they all were, partying with beer I don't buy, playing CDs I don't own on my stereo and having the time of their lives on my boat!

How could this have happened, how could they have gotten away with it? In our marina? More pictures told the story. Fortunately there were a few shots snapped in the cockpit. It seems this party was too big to all fit down in the cabin at once. From the backgrounds, I could see they were still in the marina, thank God they didn't leave the dock! But the boats were half gone and those that were there were all buttoned up tight. In the background of one shot I could see the sign in the yard of the Catholic church across the road: Bingo! Well, they only have bingo on Wednesday nights

Stupid Boat Tricks

there, so that answered one question.

In another shot, the tree next to the picnic table across the canal had no leaves: off season, fall or spring. I was getting close. But it was the third shot that zeroed it in for me. There were three girls, one of them my daughter, all holding up their right hands to the camera and pointing to brand new school class rings with the ends of their longneck beer bottles...spring, her sophomore year, about a full year before!

Well, here I was with undeniable proof that my daughter had hosted an illicit beer party aboard my boat on a weeknight when she should have been at the library. If she had had a T-Bird, I would have taken it away (sorry). I showed the photos to my wife and then...put them back into the envelope and waited for my daughter to come home.

We casually sat at the kitchen table as she walked into the room.

"Your pictures are back," I mumbled as I tossed the envelope out on the table near her. "You mother and I already went through them...there's some interesting shots in there." I can be so good at faking disinterest when I want to!

She sat down, opened up the envelope and started to flip through the snap shots.

"Oooh, ahhh," she said as she flipped through the train shots. "That's a good one! Oh, look at that one! And—" She stopped in mid sentence as she came to the one of her with the beer bottle. "Oh...I wonder who took that..." She looked at us in shear panic.

"Oh, I don't know," I said, "probably one of the dozen teenagers on my boat that night..." And I just let it hang there in the air like an unexploded grenade.

"I can explain—" she started, but I kindly never let her finish.

At that point, she could only work herself in deeper. To make a long story short, she didn't get the van that weekend. Yes, we punished her, but not as severely as we would have had the infraction not been over a year old. But how do you punish someone for something they did so long ago? And again, how can you let it go?

We compromised. While her grounding was limited, the worst part of her punishment turned out to be the number of people we have shared this story with.

"Hey, my daughter threw a secret beer bash on our boat, she actually took pictures of the incriminating evidence…and then asked her father to develop the film!"

Yeah, I guess this qualifies as a stupid boat trick all right…